Headed For Dixie and Trouble

Dr. Will L. Wade (circa 1895)

Headed for Dixie and Trouble

The Civil War Journal of Will L. Wade

EDITED WITH AN
INTRODUCTION AND NOTES
BY
Ronald Cannon

HERITAGE BOOKS
2012

HERITAGE BOOKS
AN IMPRINT OF HERITAGE BOOKS, INC.

Books, CDs, and more—Worldwide

For our listing of thousands of titles see our website at
www.HeritageBooks.com

Published 2012 by
HERITAGE BOOKS, INC.
Publishing Division
100 Railroad Ave. #104
Westminster, Maryland 21157

Copyright © 2012 Ronald Cannon

All rights reserved. No part of this book may be reproduced or transmitted in any form or by any means, electronic or mechanical, including photocopying, recording or by any information storage and retrieval system without written permission from the author, except for the inclusion of brief quotations in a review.

International Standard Book Numbers
Paperbound: 978-0-7884-5400-4
Clothbound: 978-0-7884-9306-5

Lovingly dedicated across the generations to Joseph and Jonathan.

Contents

Introduction xi

Acknowledgments xxiii

Chapter 1   "All in good spirits"
               The New Volunteer
               September to November 1861   3

Chapter 2   "Learning something about
               the art of war"
               Benton Barracks
               November and December 1861   9

Chapter 3   "We hope to down the secesh
               by spring"
               Winter Quarters in Missouri
               December 1861 to March 1862   13

Chapter 4   "Bullits were zipping close to us"
               The Road to Shiloh
               March and April 1862   31

Chapter 5   "Marched for Corinth"
               Operations in Tennessee
               and Mississippi
               April 1862 to January 1863   43

Chapter 6   "Mosquitoes more to be
               dreaded than rebs"
               The Vicksburg Campaign
               January to July 1863   55

Chapter 7	"Plenty of peaches and green corn" The March to Jackson *July 1863*	81
Chapter 8	"We are taking our ease" In camp at Vicksburg *July and August 1863*	85
Chapter 9	"Our company is pretty well played out" The Shreveport March *August and September 1863*	89
Chapter 10	"We are very comfortably situated just now" Vicksburg *September to December 1863*	93
Chapter 11	Filling the Gap: the Meridian Expedition and the Iowa Battalion *January to May 1864*	109
Chapter 12	"A Storm of Shot and Shell" The Atlanta Campaign *May to August 1864*	113
Chapter 13	"Started after Hood" Last Marches and Mustering Out *August to October 1864*	125
Appendix A	"Bald Knob: the part taken by Crocker's Iowa Brigade," from *The National Tribune*, 3 July 1884.	133
Appendix B	Roster of Company G, Eleventh Iowa Infantry	135

Bibliography 165

Index 173

Illustrations

Dr. Will L. Wade	*Frontispiece*
Captain Samuel McFarland	4
Colonel William Hall	8
Arch S. Campbell	11
Colonel Abraham M. Hare	15
Samuel Merrill Jessup	24
Levi Jessup	25
Battle of Shiloh	39
Wade Matthews	57
USS Maria Denning	61
Lt. Colonel John C. Abercrombie	64
"Adjutant General Thomas addressing the Negroes in Louisiana"	65
Jonathan Jessup	69
Emily Snoddy	83
Solon R. Jessup	86

Robert D. Wade	94
Major George Pomutz	95
Dr. William Matthews	101
Picket Station near Atlanta	121
Lee and Gordon's Mills	131

Introduction

Like many soldiers in the Civil War, Private Will L. Wade of Company G, Eleventh Regiment of Iowa Volunteer Infantry was not only literate but made use of his writing ability to keep a diary while in the army. His account begins with his enlistment in 1861 and ends as he traveled home after his discharge in 1864. Will's enthusiasm for military service cooled as time went on. Though he fulfilled his three year obligation, he had no desire to extend his service by re-enlisting. It is evident in the journal that he was marking time, particularly as time passed. He showed no strong opinions about such matters as Union and Emancipation, but merely reported events. At times he seemed almost detached, preferring to sit in camp and read, or to attend religious services. Like all soldiers, his diet took up a great deal of his interest. Also of concern was his correspondence, almost exclusively with family members. Will Wade's journal reveals an average soldier who did his duty, but who increasingly looked to his life beyond the army.

The Life of Dr. Will L. Wade

William Levi Wade was born 17 September 1841 at Stilesville, Hendricks County, Indiana. He was the second of the four children of Dr. David and Emily (Jessup) Wade. He had one older sister, Amelia, born about 1840, a younger brother Robert, born in 1848, and a younger sister, Annie, born in 1853. Will's father was a native of Frederick County, Virginia and had come to Indiana about 1836. Sometime after coming to Indiana David Wade, originally a store clerk, took up the practice of medicine. He married Will's mother, Emily Jessup, in 1838.[1] In politics he was a Whig, serving in the Indiana House of Representatives in 1848-1849. Dr. Wade evidently suffered from depression. He was admitted to the Indiana Hospital for the Insane for "melancholy"

---

[1] Hendricks County, Indiana. Marriage Records, 2:38, Wade-Jessup marriage, 1838. The marriage license was issued 30 November 1838, but no return for the actual marriage is recorded.

on 8 December 1849 and remained there for almost a year until 31 October 1850.[2] Then in January 1853 he committed suicide by taking an overdose of opium, which the local newspaper attributed to his "melancholy and perhaps mental aberration."[3]

Will's mother, Emily Jessup, was born in 1819 in Surry County, North Carolina, the eldest of the eight children of Levi and Jemima (Unthank) Jessup. Levi Jessup was a member of the Society of Friends, or Quakers, who, with Jemima and two small children, joined the migration from North Carolina to Indiana in the early 1820s. He was an early settler of Hendricks County, serving as clerk of the circuit court for seven years and being elected to the Indiana Senate for the 1831-1833 term. Levi Jessup ran for office as an anti-Jackson man, later becoming a Whig, and eventually a "radical" Republican. While in Indiana the family drifted from the tenets of the Society of Friends.[4] Indeed, Emily was complained of for non-attendance and for deviation from plainness in dress and address (or speech) in October 1838, and disowned two months later, in part for marrying the non-Quaker Dr. Wade.[5] Levi remained in Indiana until 1850 when he moved to Henry County, Iowa with his wife, Jemima, and unmarried children: William, Jonathan, Merrill, Oliver and Solon.[6]

Will Wade's early years were spent in the area of Stilesville in Hendricks County. Among his associates was his cousin David Wade Matthews (known as Wade), the son of his mother's younger sister Ruth Ann, and three years his junior.

---

[2] Dr. David Wade entry, transcript of admission book, Indiana State Hospital for the Insane, Indiana State Archives, Indianapolis, Indiana.

[3] David Wade death notice, *Danville Advertiser* (Danville, Indiana), 2, c. 3.

[4] "Levi Jessup," MS, William Hayden English Collection, M 0098, Series 6, Box 50, Folder 3; Indiana Historical Society, Indianapolis.

[5] Willard Heiss, editor, *Abstracts of the Records of the Society of Friends in Indiana*, 6 pts. (Indianapolis: Indiana Historical Society, 1962-1975), 6:183.

[6] 1850 U.S. census, Henry County, Iowa, population schedule, Jefferson township, Div. 2, p. 217 (stamped), dwelling 813, family 813, Levi Jessup; NARA microfilm publication M432, roll 184.

Wade Matthews' father was also a physician, Dr. William Matthews of Putnam County, Indiana. Ruth Ann passed away when Wade was two, and Dr. Matthews and his son migrated to Effingham County, Illinois in 1858.[7]

After her husband's death, Emily Wade took her young family and moved to Iowa, joining the rest of her family. Will attended common school in Henry County, and probably attended Howe's Academy in the county seat of Mt. Pleasant, as did his brother Robert. The academy was established by Samuel Luke Howe in 1841 as the Mount Pleasant High School and Female Seminary, and it was said that "the students in Prof. Howe's school drew in Abolitionism with their Latin and their mathematics."[8] Several members of Will's regiment, the Eleventh Iowa Infantry, had also attended Howe's school.

Emily was married again in Henry County, on 30 August 1861, to George W. Snoddy of Morgan County, Indiana.[9] Snoddy had been born in Kentucky in 1815, came to Indiana in 1822 and to Hendricks County in 1831. Emily had undoubtedly known him before she went to Iowa. Like Dr. Wade, he was a member of the Disciples of Christ and had served in the state legislature.[10] Shortly after her marriage, Emily returned with Snoddy to Indiana, taking along her youngest child Annie, who died there in 1873 at the age of twenty.[11]

---

[7] "William Matthews, M.D.," in William Henry Perrin, *History of Effingham County, Illinois* (Chicago: O. L. Baskin, 1883), 164.

[8] *History of Henry County, Iowa* (Chicago: Western Historical Co., 1879), 430, 450.

[9] Henry County, Iowa, Marriage Records, E:82, Snoddy-Wade marriage, 1861. 1860 U.S. census, Morgan County, Indiana, population schedule, Adams township, Stilesville post office, p. 818, dwelling 466, family 462, George W. Snoddy; NARA microfilm publication M653, roll 284.

[10] Shepard, et al., *A Biographical Directory of the Indiana General Assembly*, 1:365.

[11] 1870 U.S. census, Hendricks County, Indiana, population schedule, Stilesville post office, p. 359 (stamped), dwelling 28, family 27, George W. Snoddy; NARA microfilm publication M593, roll 322. *Cemetery Records, Franklin Township*.

Emily's son Robert seems to have accompanied his mother to Indiana, but by about 1863 he was clerking in a store in Wadesville, Clarke County, Virginia, probably with his uncle Daniel Wade.[12] Robert was reportedly back in Indiana by 1869, though he was living with Will in Illlinois at the time of the 1870 census. Robert went to California in 1874 and was in Los Angeles by 1878.

Will remained in Iowa when his mother remarried and moved to Indiana, having likely already decided to join the army. He probably stayed with either his grandfather, Levi, or his uncle William Jessup until he enlisted on 13 September 1861. Will's sixteen year old cousin Wade Matthews had already enlisted in Illinois a month and a half earlier. Two weeks after Will's enlistment, his uncle Jonathan Jessup enlisted in the Fourth Iowa Cavalry. Will would run across both Wade and Jonathan while in the service. Will's motivation for enlisting was probably based as much on his youthful desire for adventure as his patriotism, or the abolitionism he may have inculcated in school. However, the influence of his grandfather, the radical Republican Levi Jessup, may have also been a significant factor. Old Levi himself, at the age of nearly seventy, enlisted in March 1862 in the Thirty-seventh Iowa Infantry, the famed "Graybeard" regiment.[13]

Will's sister Amelia apparently also remained in Henry County. She was married there in February 1865 to Dearborn

---

Hendricks County, Indiana (Danville, Ind.: County Seat Genealogical Society, 2004), 80.

[12] "Robert D. Wade," in James M. Guinn, *Historical and Biographical Record of Los Angeles and Vicinity* (Chicago: Chapman, 1901), 626-627. In 1860 forty-eight year old Daniel Wade, a merchant and farmer, lived near Wadesville (1860 U.S. census, Clarke County, Virginia, population schedule, Wadesville post office, p. 597, dwelling 4, family 4, Daniel Wade; NARA microfilm publication M653, roll 1341). 1870 U.S census, Effingham County, Illinois, population schedule, Mason township, Mason Post Office, p. 468 (stamped), dwelling 243, family 246, Will L Wade; NARA microfilm publication M593, roll 219.

[13] Compiled service record, Levi Jessup, Pvt., Co. H, 37th Iowa Inf., Carded records, Volunteer Organizations, Civil War; Records of the Adjutant General's Office, 1780s-1917, Record Group 94, National Archives, Washington, D.C.

McClure. As was the case with her father, Amelia suffered some mental instability. On 3 October 1866 she was admitted to the Iowa State Hospital for the Insane at Mt. Pleasant, after an attempted suicide. The report made at the time of her admission indicates that she had suffered an "attack of insanity" six years previously. Amelia remained at the hospital for nearly fifteen years and was discharged 19 April 1881 as "not improved."[14] In 1885 she was a resident of the county poor farm.[15] She probably remained in the county facility in Mt. Pleasant until her death sometime after 1905.[16]

After his discharge from the army in 1864 Will joined his cousin Wade Matthews at Mason, Effingham County, Illinois, where they began farming together.[17] Both Will and cousin Wade married at Mason. Will married Mary Elizabeth Leith, daughter of Isaac Lowery and Francis Brown Leith, on 11 August 1866.[18] The following year Wade Matthews married Mary's sister Fannie on 24 October 1867.[19] While growing fruit in Effingham County, Illinois, Will began to read medicine, probably with Wade's father

---

[14] Amelia McClure medical file, 1866-1881, No. 839; Iowa State Hospital for the Insane, Mt. Pleasant, Iowa.

[15] 1885 Iowa state census, Henry County, Iowa, population schedule, Center township, p. 123, line 11, Amelia McClure; digital image, Iowa State Census Collection, 1836-1925 (http://www.ancestry.com : accessed 1 October 2008).

[16] 1905 Iowa state census, Henry County, Mt. Pleasant, line 313, roll IA_90; digital image, Iowa State Census Collection, 1836-1925 (http://www.ancestry.com : accessed 28 October 2008).

[17] "David Wade Matthews," *History of Effingham County*, 166.

[18] Effingham County, Illinois, marriages, B:175, Wade-Leith marriage, 1866. William L. Wade (Pvt., Co. G, 11th Ia. Inf., Civil War), pension no. Inv.1,085,581, Case Files of Approved Pension Applications...,1861-1934; Civil War and Later Pension Files; Department of Veterans Affairs, Record Group 15; National Archives, Washington, D.C.

[19] Effingham County, Illinois, marriages, B:98, Mathews-Leith marriage, 1867. Fannie A. Matthews, widow's pension no. 762835; Civil War, RG 15, NA-Washington.

Dr. William Matthews. His interest in a medical career was probably of long standing since it is already evident in his journal. Will and Mary Wade migrated to Oregon in the spring of 1875 and took up residence in the community of Shedds (now Shedd) in Linn County. Will's uncle Dr. Solon R. Jessup had lived in Oregon since 1863, graduating in 1868 from the medical department of Willamette University in Salem. Will returned east briefly in 1879 to complete his medical training at Butler University in Indianapolis. Upon his return to Oregon Will settled in Salem where he practiced medicine and was a member of the Oregon State Medical Society, though not as its president as has been stated.[20] He may also have spent six years as the medical officer of the Oregon State Penitentiary in Salem. In 1881 cousin Wade Matthews followed Will to Oregon and also settled in Salem.[21]

Will left Oregon in the spring of 1887 for Los Angeles, California. He moved to Los Angeles presumably for health reasons. This was evidently a wise move as he lived for over forty more years. Will maintained a medical practice in Los Angeles, as well as lectured at the University of Southern California.[22] Will and Robert's mother, Emily, also came to Los Angeles by at least 1885 when Amelia's daughter Emma was married there.[23]

---

[20] Dr. Mae H. Cardwell, "The Oregon State Medical Society -- an Historical Sketch," *Medical Sentinel*, v. 13, no. 7 (July 1905), 199. "Will L. Wade," *An Illustrated History of Los Angeles County, California*, (Chicago: Lewis Publishing Co., 1889), 233.

[21] "David Wade Matthews," in William Henry Perrin, *History of Effingham County, Illinois* (Chicago: O. L. Baskin & Co., 1883) 165-166.

[22] "Will L. Wade," *An Illustrated History of Los Angeles County, California*, 233. 1880 U.S. census, Marion County, Oregon, population schedule, Salem Pct., ED 78, p. 1 (stamped), dwelling 17, family 17, Wel L. Wade; NARA microfilm publication T9, roll 1082. 1900 U.S. census, Los Angeles County, California, population schedule, Los Angeles City, ED 24, p. 57-B (stamped), sheet 5, dwelling 69, family 116, William L. Wade; NARA microfilm publication T623, roll 89.

[23] Los Angeles County, California, marriage book 10:268. Poindexter-Jessup marriage (1885); see also marriage notice. *Los Angeles Times*, 2 May 1885.

Will's wife, Mary, passed away 9 October 1909 at Los Angeles.[24] On 15 September 1911 the seventy year old Will married a fifty-nine year old widow, Mrs. Adelaide Huntley MacGregor.[25] This marriage was not destined to last, however, as Will and Adelaide had separated by 1920.[26] Then, at the age of nearly eighty, Will did some traveling abroad and by 1924 had purchased a craftsman house in South Pasadena.

About 1927 Will married for the third and final time. His bride was the sixty year old Mrs. Ida Blethen. Ida was a native of Minnesota and the widow of Henry Blethen, with whom she had one daughter, Grace. The Blethens had lived in Louisiana before coming to California about 1904. Will and Ida lived together at his South Pasadena home until Will passed away 18 February 1931. Ida remained in South Pasadena until her own death 14 November 1946.[27]

The Journal

---

[24] Los Angeles County (California) death certificate no. 3204, Mary E. Wade (1909).

[25] William L. Wade Civil War pension no. 1085581, RG 15, NA-Washington.

[26] 1920 U.S. census, Los Angeles County, California, population schedule, Los Angeles City, Pct. 427, ED 180, p. 152-B (stamped), sheet 14, dwelling 328, family 337, Adelaide Wade; NARA microfilm publication T625, roll 107. 1920 U.S. census, Los Angeles County, California, population schedule, Los Angeles City, ED 236, p. 190-B (stamped), sheet 7, dwelling 8, family 8, William L Waden [sic]; NARA microfilm publication T626, roll 109. 1930 U.S. census, Los Angeles County, California, population schedule, South Pasadena City, ED 19-1525, p. 268-B (stamped), sheet 4, dwelling 112, family 117, Will & Ida Wade; NARA microfilm publication T626, roll 175.

[27] 1900 U.S. census, Calcasieu Parish, Louisiana, population schedule, Ward 3, Lake Charles City, enumeration district (ED) 16, p. 145-B (stamped), sheet 13, dwelling 235, family 237, Harry McCleery; NARA microfilm publication T623, roll 560. 1930 U.S. census, Los Angeles County, California, population schedule, South Pasadena City, ED 19-1525, p. 268-B (stamped), sheet 4, dwelling 112, family 117, Will & Ida Wade; NARA microfilm publication T626, roll 175. Los Angeles County, California, death certificate no. 1206, Will Levi Wade (1931). Los Angeles County, California death certificate no. 13383, Ida Blethem Wade (1946).

Since Will had no children, after his death all his effects passed to his widow Ida. Her daughter, Grace Blethen Dunn, came into possession of the journal at least by the time of Ida's death in 1946. The journal remained with Grace Blethen Dunn and was passed to her descendants and is currently in the possession of her granddaughter, Jane Dunn Kolb of Mandeville, Louisiana. There are extant copies of an earlier transcription of the journal, located in various repositories, however this work is based on a new transcription of the original manuscript.[28]

The journal consists of one hundred thirty-seven numbered pages of a single-volume lined record book. The pages measure seven and one half by nine and one half inches. Inside the front cover of the journal Grace Dunn taped a notice, which reads:

Diary of Dr. Will L. Wade
Born in Stilesville, Indiana, of
Quaker stock, Sept. 17, 1841
Died Feb. 18, 1930. [sic]
When the War Between the States
broke out, he enlisted in the
11th Iowa Infantry, serving in
Company G. to the end of the war.
About 1886 he became Professor
of Materia Medica and Secretary
of the Faculty at the College
of Medicine of the University
of Southern California at Los Angeles.
He copied his diary, written
during the war, into this record
book to preserve it. It is in his
own handwriting.
  Authenticated by his
  stepdaughter

---

[28] Transcriptions are located, for example, in the archival collection of the Center for Southeast Louisiana Studies at Southeastern Louisiana University and in the Civil War Miscellaneous Collection at the U.S. Army Military History Institute.

Mrs. Grace Blethen Dunn

    Will probably kept his original record in the small pocket sized pre-dated diaries widely available at the time. There is nothing indicating when Will might have recopied his journal. There is a photograph of him stapled to the beginning of the record book which shows him in his fifties or possibly sixties. He may have felt the need to preserve the record in conjunction with his first application for a pension based on his military service in 1904.[29] It would seem likely that he transferred the record sometime between 1890 and 1904, after he had moved to Los Angeles.

    Grace Dunn's comments about his preserving the journal indicate that the original diaries may have deteriorated, or were deteriorating. This is understandable given the poor circumstances under which they would have been produced in camp and on the march. It is also possible that they were not stored under the best of conditions over the years, particularly in the damp climate of Oregon's Willamette Valley. There are several gaps in the record, most notably a month between 18 June and 28 July 1862, three months from 5 October 1862 to the end of the year, and a nearly six month gap between 31 December 1863 and 29 June 1864. It appears that Will had lost some of the originals and had planned to fill in the gaps, since he left blank pages between (about twenty pages in all). The handwriting of the journal is quite legible and the spelling is good by modern standards. This reflects either Will's education or the fact that he was recopying the journal as a mature adult, or both.

    There are several instances where Will evidently was unable to read clearly what was written in the originals. He seems to have had particular trouble with the names of railroads. While for the most part he appears to have copied the original entries faithfully, there are some instances when he includes information that he could only have learned later. Other editing may have taken place when, for example, he referred to a young lady in Iowa whom he corresponded with merely by her initials, a discretionary

---

[29] William L. Wade Civil War pension no. 1085581, RG 15, NA-Washington.

move for a married man. Whether mere coincidence or an indication of some more selective editing, it is interesting that the longest gap in the journal begins on the day Will was reduced in rank.

Most known war records by members of the Eleventh Iowa are by Veteran Volunteers, soldiers who re-enlisted beyond their initial three year commitment. These men all received a thirty day furlough in the late winter and spring of 1864. Most notable are the published accounts of Mifflin Jennings of Company C, William S. Fultz of Company D, Alexander G. Downing of Company E, Daniel J. Parvin of Company H and William Burge of Company K. Burge wrote and published his eighty-one page account sometime before his death in 1907. Mostly anecdotal in nature, Burge probably based his book on his diaries, as he did give some specific dates associated with the events he described. Fultz composed a two hundred page detailed history of Company D about 1885, based on his own diaries and letters he received from comrades. It remains mostly in manuscript form, but a version edited by Mildred Throne in 1957 was published in the *Iowa Journal of History*. Throne included only the "highlights" and left out of her edition descriptions of camp life and marches that she considered "dreary reading." The most complete account is that of Alex Downing. Published in 1916, it purports to be a direct transcription of his wartime diary. Jennings' diary remains in manuscript form, though a transcript is available on the Internet. The narrative begins in November 1862, with regular daily entries starting in late April 1863. Most recently available are the 117 wartime letters of Daniel Parvin. Rather than a strict chronological presentation, Parvin's letters, edited by his great-great grandson, are arranged topically.[30]

---

[30] Diaries of Mifflin Jennings, Co. C, Eleventh Iowa Infantry, originals in the possession of Ronald D. Smith, Larned, Kansas (http://www.rootsweb.ancestry.com ; accessed 23 September 2010); William S. Fultz, "A History of Company D, Eleventh Iowa Infantry Volunteers," Special Collections, Iowa State Historical Society, Iowa City, Iowa; Mildred Throne, (ed.), "A History of Company D, Eleventh Iowa Infantry, 1861-1865," *Iowa Journal of History*, v. 55, no. 1 (January 1957), 35-90; Olynthus B. Clark, ed., *Downing's Civil War Diary* (Des Moines: Historical Department of Iowa, 1916);

Will's journal, on the other hand, reflects the experience of the non-veteran. He allowed his term of service to expire before the end of the conflict and left for home while his regiment was still in the field. Though he had experienced the major battles and campaigns of Shiloh, Vicksburg and Atlanta, he left before the regiment participated in Sherman's march to the sea and the campaign through the Carolinas. While the veterans were on furlough, Will and the other non-veterans from Iowa had been combined together to form the Iowa Battalion. Unfortunately, the greatest gap occurring in his journal covers this period. As a result, his whereabouts and activities must be reconstructed from other sources. Particularly useful in this regard is the memoir of William Henry Jennings of Company C. The younger brother of Mifflin Jennings, William Jennings was a later recruit and joined the regiment in March 1864, remaining with the Iowa Battalion when the veterans went on furlough.[31]

While what remains of Will Wade's journal is not complete, and his style is somewhat terse, it is still a valuable contribution to the perspective of a private soldier in the Civil War and, in particular, to the history of the Eleventh Iowa.

Phillip A. Hubbart, ed., *An Iowa Soldier Writes Home: the Civil War Letters of Union Private Daniel J. Parvin* (Durham, N.C.: Carolina Academic Press, 2011); William Burge, *Through the Civil War and Western Adventures* (Lisbon, Ia.: W. Burge, n. d.).

[31] William Henry Jennings, *My Story* (Fremont, Neb.: Hammond Printing Co., c. 1915).

Acknowledgments

There have been many individuals whose help and cooperation have been essential to the publication of this Civil War journal. I would like to thank Reuben Dunn of Whittier, California, for bringing the manuscript's existence to my attention. Jane Kolb of Mandeville, Louisiana, the owner of the manuscript, was very gracious in allowing me access to the original journal.

Others have contributed significantly to the quality of this work. Jananne Slaughter of Lone Tree, Iowa was invaluable in obtaining a copy the manuscript of William S. Fultz of Company D located in the State Historical Society of Iowa. She also contributed Jessup family photos. Becki Plunkett of the State Historical Society of Iowa was helpful in obtaining images of Will Wade's commanders from the Loren Tyler Collection of Military Photographs. Other images of Wade family members were provided by the great-grandchildren of Will's brother Robert, namely, Nina Anderson of Flagstaff, Arizona, and Vance Gustafson of San Diego, California.

Headed For Dixie and Trouble

Chapter I
"All in Good Spirits"
The New Volunteer
September to November 1861

When President Abraham Lincoln called for the raising of 75,000 volunteers on 15 April 1861, Iowa responded immediately by raising what became the First Iowa Volunteer Infantry. This ninety-day regiment was mustered in 14 May and mustered out on 20 August 1861. In the meantime, President Lincoln had issued a call for an additional 300,000 three-year enlistments on 3 May. Since nearly ten regiments of Iowa volunteers had answered Lincoln's first request, the Second through Tenth Iowa regiments were then mustered into service between May and September 1861.[1] Enlistments continued throughout the fall of 1861 and several more regiments continued to be formed. These regiments were initially raised by the state of Iowa, but were subsequently sworn into Federal service. Will Wade enlisted as a member of what soon became Company G, Eleventh Iowa Regiment of Volunteer Infantry.

1861   Mt Pleasant Iowa

Sept 13   To day I volunteered under Capt McFarland and was sworn into the State Service.[2] Have been walking around town most of the time getting acquainted with the boys. We are quartered at the

---

[1] S. H. M. Byers, *Iowa in War Times* (Des Moines: W. D. Condit, 1888), 481-500.

[2] Samuel McFarland, a Pennsylvania born attorney from Mt. Pleasant, was the first captain of Company G, but later became a lieutenant colonel in the Nineteenth Iowa. See Appendix B.

Brazelton House about twenty men mostly young.³

Captain Samuel McFarland (State Historical Society of Iowa)

14 Walking the streets, eating fruit, Some talking as to who all to be officers Geo. W. Barr (First Iowa) is mentioned for Lieut C. B. Weir for orderly Sergt.⁴

15 After polishing up, G. W. Barr and I attended the Baptist church. I have felt very lonely since my folks went East but now feel a little more like myself.

---

³ The Brazelton House Hotel, located at 100 North Main Street, Mt. Pleasant, is no. 86002700 on the National Register of Historic Places.

⁴ George W. F. Barr, who had previously served in the First Iowa Infantry, and Caleb W. Weir. See Appendix B.

	16	Company drilled part of the day in the hall. There are now fifty men. We were told that we start for Camp McClellan Davenport tomorrow morning.[5]
[Sept]	17	After goodbyes to friends we boarded cars for Burlington just as Capt Jones men got off.[6] Boys were lively cheering and whooping it up all the way. Board boat just at dark, and sat down to a hard supper. My "Birth day anniversary[.]"
Sept	18	Most of us slept very poorly last night A number were playing cards and made so much noise that sleep was impossible. During the day we steamed slowly up the river. All in good spirits. Arrived at camp about 2.
[Sept]	19	Today we have been looking for Davenport, at last at about 8 AM it came into view. The tall flagstaff of the camp marking its location on the

---

[5] Camp McClellan was established at Davenport in August 1861 by Adjutant General Nathaniel B. Baker (see Seth Temple, "Camp McClellan during the Civil War," *Annals of Iowa*, 21:1[July 1937], 17-55).

[6] This was apparently a company of local militia that had gone to northern Missouri to assist Colonel David Moore of the First Northeastern Missouri Home Guard in the action against Colonel Martin Green of the Missouri State Guard (Confederate) at Athens, Missouri. The "boys" from Henry County may have gone in July, and were probably just returning as Will and his comrades left for Camp McClellan at Davenport. See "Hon. George McNeeley," *A Memorial and Biographical Record of Iowa Illustrated* (Chicago: Lewis Publishing Co., 1896), 31. For the engagement at Athens, see Jonathan K. Cooper-Wiele, *Skim Milk Yankees Fighting: the Battle of Athens, Missouri, August 5, 1861* (Iowa City: Camp Pope Bookshop, 2007). "Capt. Jones" probably refers to Warren C. Jones (1828-1878), of Mt. Pleasant, who was subsequently captain of Company I, Fourteenth Iowa Infantry (Warren C. Jones, *Organization Index to Pension Files of Veterans who served between 1861 and 1900*, Record Group 15, NARA microfilm publication T289; Iowa Adjutant General's Office, *Roster and Record of Iowa Soldiers in the War of the Rebellion*, 6vols. (Des Moines, 1908-1911), 2:818; 1860 U.S. census, Henry Co., Iowa, pop. sch., Marion twp., Mt. Pleasant p.o., p. 327, dwel. 71, fam. 72, W C Jones; NARA micro. publ. T653, roll 324).

bluff very plainly we came rapidly up to the landing and about 9 we were ashore and marching to camp about two miles distant.

Will's journal is spotty for the next two months, with only six entries between 19 September and 27 November. He left space to be filled in later, indicating that the originals were probably either lost or in an illegible state. A comparison with other sources indicates that as Will attempted to reconstruct this period he was somewhat off as to exact dates. Nevertheless, most of Will's time during this period was spent in learning how to be a soldier, particularly in practicing the intricacies of drilling.[7]

Oct 14 To day our company marched down town to be mustered into United States service after waiting around nearly all day. And then marched back to camp without anything being done. The boys laid the blame on Capt Alex Chambers of the Regular army, mustering officer at this point.[8] I was sick at the time, and rode down in a carriage.

Oct 15 After more or less of an examination during which several were rejected, one or two because their patriotism had had a chance to cool a little, and who found out that their parents were "not willing" were dropped out. A few who were very young asked older men to stand up and answer as their names were called, then all raised their right

---

[7] See *Downing's Civil War Diary*, 9-17.

[8] Alexander Chambers (1833-1888), a West Point graduate and assigned to the Fifth U.S. Infantry, became colonel of the Sixteenth Iowa Infantry and later commanded the Third Division in the XVII Army Corps ("General Alexander Chambers," *Iowa Historical Record* 9:1 [January 1893], 385-393; see also Ezra J. Warner, *Generals in Blue: Lives of the Union Commanders* [Louisiana State University Press, 1964], 77-78).

hands and swore to stand by the country for three years unless sooner discharged.[9]

Oct 26 Our clothing and accoutrements arrived and will be distributed tomorrow.

Oct 27 Our uniforms and accoutrements were issued this morning, and gave rise to a lot of fun. Some of the little fellows had to roll up their sleeves and trousers, while others had to coax theirs down. We drew tall felt hats with lots of brass on them, eagles and trumpets, feathers and cords. There were brass shoulder straps, and cross breast straps.[10]

Nov 13 To day, after we had spent the first two days in drilling, we marched as a regiment to attend the funeral of Lieut Col. August Wentz of the 7" Iowa, who was killed at the battle of Belmont, when the 7" was so badly cut up.[11] The 11" Iowa.

---

[9] Company D was sworn in on 3 October and Company E on 5 October (Fultz, 39; *Downing's Civil War Diary*, 12). It is likely that Will's Company G was mustered in on 5 not 15 October. His record has significant gaps on either side of these two entries indicating the originals were missing or difficult to read. However, his company muster-in roll was dated 4 November 1861 (Compiled service record, William L. Wade, Pvt., Co. G, 11th Iowa Inf., Carded records, Volunteer Organizations, Civil War; Records of the Adjutant General's Office, 1780s-1917, Record Group 94, National Archives, Washington, D.C.).

[10] Fultz states that Company D received uniforms on 26 October, haversacks, knapsacks and canteens on 27 October and guns and accoutrements on 29 October (Fultz, 40). Downing indicates that the uniforms for the regiment were received on 31 October and distribution began on 1 November, Company E drawing theirs on 2 November (*Downing's Civil War Diary*, 15-16).

[11] Augustus Wentz was born at Koenigsbach, Baden in 1829, migrated to the United States in 1845 and served in the Second U.S. Artillery during the Mexican War ("Lieut.-Col. Augustus Wentz, Iowa Vol.," in John Gilmary Shea, *A Child's History of the United States* [New York: MacDavitt, 1872], 2:416-418). The Battle of Belmont in Mississippi County, Missouri was fought on 7 November 1861. It was significant in that it proved to be the first combat action for General

13" Iowa and cavalry formed the escort. All went pretty well except the firing which sputtered a little. Lieut Col Billy Hall who commanded the 11" exclaimed "Eleventh Iowa I am proud of you"[12]

Colonel William Hall (State Historical Society of Iowa)

Ulysses S. Grant (see David J. Eicher, *The Longest Night: a Military History of the Civil War* [New York: Simon & Schuster, 2001], 142-145).

[12] William Hall (1832-1866), a Canadian born lawyer from Davenport, was originally the Eleventh's major, being promoted to lieutenant colonel 11 October 1861. He became colonel of the regiment after the Battle of Shiloh (A. A. Stuart, *Iowa Colonels and Regiments* (Des Moines: Mills, 1865), 237-242; 1860 U.S. census, Scott County, Iowa, population schedule, Davenport, p. 224, dwelling 721, family 654, Wm Hall; NARA microfilm publication M653, roll 340).

Chapter II
"Learning Something about the Art of War"
Benton Barracks
November and December 1861

After their initial training at Camp McClellan near Davenport, the soldiers in the Eleventh were transported to Benton Barracks near St. Louis, Missouri. Benton Barracks was a Union Army camp of instruction and was named by General John C. Fremont for his father in law, the late Senator Thomas H. Benton.[1] As at Davenport, Will and his regiment spent much of their time in drilling and learning camp duties.

Nov 16   We are under orders at last to go down the river to St Louis. The order was received with much enthusiasm. We packed up and marched down to the landing, going on board the Jennie Whipple and barges. The weather is fresh and cool and our quarters not very comfortable.

By the time the Eleventh arrived at St. Louis on 19 November, the weather had turned disagreeable. The soldiers marched into camp in the pouring rain.[2] As winter was approaching, the Eleventh were issued overcoats on 23 November.[3]

Nov 27   Camp Benton. I have just written home. My letters seem few and far between. We have been

---

[1] Lieut. S[eymour] D[wight] Thompson, *Recollections with the Third Iowa Regiment* (Cincinnati, 1864), 169.

[2] *Downing's Civil War Diary* 19; Fultz MS, 8. See also, *Roster and Record*, 2:275

[3] Fultz MS. 8.

in this camp one week and are learning something about the art of war. We drill almost every day. Weather is clear and cool. Iowa regiments are coming in to form Curtis Brigade.[4] News is encouraging. Our troops have won in some engagements. I am quite well.

Nov 28 Nothing of importance occurred today. It is quite cool and raw. There are many sick in camp just now, 10 to 20 in each company.

Nov 29 Today we have been pitching our tents.[5] I am with Campbell, Gaskill, Turney and Lowry.[6] We are not sleeping out yet. It is too cool. The 2^d-3^d-7"-11"-12-13 Iowa Regt's are here and others are expected soon.

---

[4] Samuel Ryan Curtis (1805-1866), veteran of the Mexican War, congressman, and colonel of the Second Iowa Infantry, was appointed brigadier general 17 May 1861. He was briefly in command of Benton Barracks (Warner, *Generals in Blue*, 107-108; Stuart, *Iowa Colonels and Regiments*, 37-38).

[5] The tents issued at this time would have been Sibley tents, tepee-likestructures with a central pole and designed to sleep up to twenty men. It was designed by Major Henry Hopkins Sibley (1816-1886) in the 1850s after the tepees he had seen on the frontier. Sibley was a brigadier general in the Confederate army during the Civil War (Webb Garrison, *The Encyclopedia of Civil War Usage: an illustrated compendium of the everyday language of soldiers and civilians* [Nashville: Cumberland House, 2001], 227; Ezra J. Warner, *Generals in Gray* [Baton Rouge: Louisiana State University Press, 1959], 276-277).

[6] Archibald S. Campbell was orphaned as a child and was living in Henry County with Will's uncle William A. Jessup in 1860 (1860 U.S. census, Henry County, Iowa, population schedule, Jefferson township, Marshall post office, p. 12, dwelling 83, family 82, W^m A Jessup; NARA microfilm publication M653, roll 324). The others were Elis Gaskill, Darius Turney and Ambrose Lowry. See Appendix B.

Arch S. Campbell
(Courtesy of Vance Gustafson)

Nov 30   Our company was out on skirmish drill some distance away from barracks this morning. After dinner they let us go out in the woods after persimmons, Frank Force found a fine lot, we also got walnuts and hickory nuts.[7] An order was read forbidding smoking in barracks.

Dec 1   Sunday is always a busy day with soldiers. I arose early and went to the First Iowa Cav for breakfast. Then marched until late in the evening, about 4 P.M. I had supper. I was hungry, cold and tired. Then I had to stay up till roll call. At the close of dress parade one of the 3^d Iowa Sergts shot and killed his bunkmate in play.[8]

Dec 2   We waked up this morning to find the ground covered with snow. Had company and Battalion drill, and parade. My feet have been cold all day. I hope to get a furlough by spring, but am not homesick, would like to see how a good bath would go over once more. So far I have eaten no

---

[7] Franklin Force was later adjutant of the Fiftieth U.S. Colored Infantry. See Appendix B.

[8] Private James McManus of Company A, Third Iowa Infantry was accidentally killed by a comrade during a mock battle on 15 November 1861 (*Roster and Record*, 1:352; Thompson, *Recollections with the Third Iowa Regiment*, 171).

pork, but have plenty to eat. Troops continue to come in there are about 15,000 here now.

Dec 3 — To day we drilled all day in the snow, although moving around pretty lively. I had cold feet all day. In the evening we went hunting persimmons, Force as usual found a fine lot in a hilly wood pasture and we all filled our haver sacks. They were very fine and ripe.

Dec 4 — I had more persimmons than I wanted yesterday and they don't look good anymore. Nothing unusual today. Battalion and Company drill. Plenty to eat and excellent bread from a general bakery.

Dec 5 — Am on guard duty today. Not feeling very well. About ten of the men have measles, Campbell for one, and their coughing keeps others awake at night.

Dec 6 — Came off guard this morning, after a pleasant night. After breakfast slept till evening.

Chapter III
"We hope to down the Secesh by Spring"
Winter Quarters in Missouri
December 1861 to March 1862

After being duly trained and instructed, the Eleventh Iowa was stationed, with other regiments, in the counties around Jefferson City, in order to maintain the authority of the Federal government and seek out Confederate troops operating in the area. By Christmas half of the regiment, under Lt. Col. Hall, was garrisoned around the town of California, in Moniteau County, while the rest, including Company G, were with Col. Hare at Fulton, in Callaway County.[1]

Dec 7   It is reported that we are to go to Jefferson City, and all are much pleased to get on the move. The Col. did not want to go without full equipment, but we got positive orders to go.

Dec 8   We are busy packing up and making ready to go. Campbell and Turney were left. I met several old friends, Dave Harland and others.[2] We went aboard Mo. Pacific [Railroad] and started for Jefferson City, we ran alongside the Missouri river much of the way. Rode in freight cars with rough seats.

Dec 9   Arrived in Jefferson City toward morning but remained on cars, at an early hour we marched to camp escorted by the 47" Ill In which I found Jas.

---

[1]*Downing's Civil War Diary*, 25-26; *History of Muscatine County, Iowa* (Chicago: Clarke, 1911), 137-141.

[2] David Harlan (1834-1916), Company F, Fourteenth Iowa Infantry, was a native of Indiana from Gainesboro(ugh) in Van Buren County ("David Harland," *Roster and Record*, 2:811; David Harlan, *Organization Index to Pension Files of Veterans who served between 1861 and 1900*).

Rowley in Co. "B."³ Our camp is half a mile west of the Capitol building, on a creek, in full view, and fortified all around. Part of the First Iowa Cav. are here.

Dec 10 We are enjoying the unusual freedom allowed us. I have been on police duty working hard. Have had no time to write. Have received no letters since leaving Iowa. Gen. MᶜKean complimented our Regiment for promptness in coming.⁴ A lot of us visited the State house. The rebel Legislature had run away. We found proclamation by Gov. Jackson calling on every body to arise and wipe the invaders out, but they skedaddled all the same.⁵

Dec 11 Most of the boys have been busy building fireplaces in their tents. Col Hare furnished the

---

[3] James F. Roley (1832-1893), Company B, Forty-seventh Illinois Infantry, was an Ohio native from Washington, Tazewell County, Illinois (*Report of the Adjutant General of the State of Illinois*, Vol. 3 [Springfield: H.W. Rokker, 1886], 414; James F. Roley, *Organization Index to Pension Files of Veterans who served between 1861 and 1900*).

[4] General Thomas Jefferson McKean (1810-1870) was a West Point graduate who curiously served as an enlisted man through the Mexican War. He spent most of the Civil War in administrative rather than field duties. He was in command at Jefferson City from December 1861 to March 1862 (Warner, *Generals in Blue*, 301; Eicher, *Civil War High Commands*, 379).

[5] Claiborne Fox Jackson (1807-1862), was a native of Kentucky and for many years served in the Missouri legislature as a States' Rights Democrat. He was elected governor in 1860, called a secession convention in 1861 which instead declared the governor's office vacant. He fled the capital and called the legislature to meet at Neosho, where it passed an ordinance of secession. He continued to flee south into Arkansas where he remained until his death (Howard L. Conard, *Encyclopedia of the History of Missouri: a Compendium of History and Biography for Ready Reference*, 6 vols.[New York: Southern History Co., 1901], 3:397-398).

brick.⁶ The Paymaster came and paid us off in gold. I sent mine home. Weather cool. I received my first letter.

Colonel Abraham M. Hare (State Historical Society of Iowa)

Dec 12 Making preparations to march, but our destination is not known. Other troops are to go with us. We think there may be some fighting. The war begins to have a more favorable appearance. We hope to down the secesh by spring.⁷

---

⁶Abraham M. Hare (1811-1903), a native of Ohio, was the regiment's first colonel. He led a brigade at Shiloh and resigned after being wounded there (Stuart, *Iowa Colonels and Regiments*, 235-236; A.M. Hare obituary, *Muscatine* [Iowa] *Journal*, 9 February 1903, p. 2, c. 1, quoted in Linda Alstrom Hare, *Seven Hares in the Civil War* [Atlanta, KS: HHR, 2005], 112-113).

⁷ Secessionists.

Dec 13 There are rumors in camp of starting on an expedition up the Missouri river. It is said that the Colonels orders are sealed.

Dec 14 This morning we are all packed up and ready to march. It keeps us busy to keep our things separated from those belonging to other companies. They kept us standing all day at the boat landing, and it was night when we finally went on board and started up the river.

Dec 15 This morning we landed at Providence and after breakfast our regiment and the cavalry started on a scouting trip[.][8] We marched about ten miles and returned at night with a lot of prisoners among them a Lieut in Price's Army.[9]

Dec 16 During Sunday night we steamed to Booneville where we crossed the river and Cos A. E. I. and G. went on a scout to Boonsborough which we occupied most of the night.[10] We thought there would be some fighting, but there was none. The cavalry took some prisoners, one was armed with a shot gun, Revolver two horsepistols and a bowie knife. We surrounded the town with picket guards.

---

[8] Providence is located in Boone County across the Missouri River from Lupus. Four companies of the Second Illinois Cavalry accompanied the Eleventh (*Downing's Civil War Diary*, 23-24).

[9] Sterling Price (1809-1867), Missouri legislator, congressman, Mexican War veteran and former governor of Missouri, was in command of the Missouri militia and was later a major general in the Confederate army (Warner, *Generals in Gray*, 246-247).

[10] Boonville is located in Cooper County and Boonesboro is across the river in Howard County.

Dec	17	In the morning we searched the houses we found two bayonets, some caps, shot, powder and rifles. We took the Postmaster and contents of the post office, a wagon two horses &c The people were ignorant and thought we had come to kill and burn. They soon found out better when a number took the oath. Our visit was rather profitable.
Dec	18	I helped this forenoon to stow away on the Steamer 172 kegs of powder found by the cavalry last night on the farm of a Col. in Price's army living near Glasgow.[11] It was hid in a haystack[.] A slave in the place told a darkey with the cavalry. It was quite a loss to the Rebs. We steamed down the river until night and then laid up.
Dec	19	During the day we made the run to Jefferson City, where we arrived without mishap and marched to camp where we fell to work putting up our tents, and before night we were in our old quarters, as if nothing had happened[.]
Dec	20	To day I was detailed as orderly at the Adjutants office, and was kept busy carrying orders, calling orderlies, keeping up fires &c. I liked the work very well.
Dec	21	This morning I was relieved from duty at the Adjutants office, and promised myself a rest. It was growing quite cold, too much so to live in tents. Our boys are busy building fireplaces for

---

[11] Probably Colonel Congreve Jackson (1860 U.S. census, Howard Co., Missouri, pop. sch., Chariton twp., Glasgow P.O., p. 505, dwel. 696, fam. 661, Congrave Jackson; NARA microfilm publ. M653, roll 623; see also John McElroy, *The Struggle for Missouri* [Washington, D.C.: National Tribune, 1909], 212). Downing counted 155 kegs of powder (*Downing's Civil War Diary*, 24).

		their tents some have bought stoves, and we are pretty warm and comfortable.
Dec	22^d	To day the ground is covered with snow and I am on guard. It is quite cold with a good stiff wind, we are not allowed any fires as there is a powder magazine on my beat. During the night half the Regt. left for California. There are 20 of our Co on duty, this puts us on every other night. Wickiger of Co. B. and myself took dinner with a German family, friends of his.[12] It was extremely good.
Dec	23	Last night was a tough one, and I am trying to get a little rest. The weather is cold for men in tents. We are beginning to feel a contempt for all Missourians.
Dec	24	It is again reported that we are to go to Fulton, as the rebels are said to be burning bridges in that vicinity.[13] We packed up during the day, but were ordered back to our tents. In the evening we packed up again and crossed the river.
Dec	25	About 15 of us including the Captain passed the night in a large fine house[.] I slept on the parlor floor. The host was very kind. We joined the other companies and took up the march for Fulton. Had much difficulty getting our wagons up some of the hills, camped at a church all night.

---

[12] Presumably Will misread his original diary. There is no "Wickiger" or "Wickizer" in any Iowa regiment, let alone Co. B of the Eleventh. Company B does have on its roster Peter Nickelson (1838-1913) from Eldora in Hardin County. A native of Pennsylvania, he may have had German friends living in Missouri (*Roster and Record*, 2:364; Peter Nickelson, *Organization Index to Pension Files of Veterans who served between 1861 and 1900*).

[13] Fulton is located in Callaway County.

Dec	26	Marched again in the morning, and after a few hours brisk tramping arrived at Fulton one of the prettiest towns in Mo. Here are located several public institutions Insane,[14] Deaf and dumb,[15] and blind Asylums. We are quartered in the deaf and dumb asylum a large brick building. We have bunks, tables, stoves, and a range for our cooking. Ordered to sleep on arms tonight.
Dec	27	To day we went on a scout to Concord about 12 miles in a northerly direction about halfway to Mexico.[16] Found no rebels, turned toward home, arrived at night very tired. We did very fine marching about five miles per hour.
Dec	28	We drew some good beef today and had a treat after eating so much pork. We have a chance to buy fruit and vegetables, and trade in the stores. This is a pleasant town with very agreeable people.
Dec	29	We fired off our guns and had the usual Sunday inspection. I got through all right. Citizens and darkies flocked in to see the sight, and watched every movement with open mouthed curiosity.

---

[14] This was the Fulton State Hospital. See Richard L. Lael, et al., *Evolution of a Missouri Asylum: Fulton State Hospital, 1851-2006* (Columbia, Mo.: University of Missouri Press, 2007).

[15] Missouri School for the Deaf, established in 1851. See Richard D. Reed, *Historic MSD: the story of the Missouri School for the Deaf* (Fulton, Mo.: Richard D. Reed, 2000).

[16] Concord was located about four miles west of modern Auxvasse in Callaway County, twelve miles north of Fulton. Mexico is in Audrain County to the north.

Dec	30	Nothing much of note, we are very comfortable in our quarters in the Asylum building[.] On guard today, are shaping up into pretty fair soldiers. Just at night had orders to march to Millersburg nearly west.[17]
Dec	31	This morning we started and arrived about noon, some 17 miles. Camped in a church, scouts found turkey, applebutter, honey &c. We had a good time. Had fires outside, and ate and told stories. While broiling chickens and turkey some one looked up and there stood Col. Hare[.] He sentenced to [the] men to give him a piece of bread and some applebutter.

1862

Jan	1	We started back to Fulton 12 miles away[.] We marched at a good rate and arrive in town at 3 P.M. fully satisfied with our tramp, it was probably to practice us in scouting. The Col. complimented Co. G. Our sick, left in Jefferson City [,] returned today.
Jan	2^d	A subscription was started and money raised to buy turkeys, they were dressed and roasted, after being filled with good dressing and we enjoyed a feast of good things. I am to nurse in the hospital tonight.
Jan	3^d	Some of the companies were out all night[,] came in during the morning bringing some prisoners.
Jan	5"	Today I attended church for the first time since enlisting. Very fair sermon. It seemed like home

---

[17] Millersburg is in Callaway County towards Columbia.

		again. Our Chaplain feels the influence of living in a dumb asylum.[18]
Jan	6"	Drilling this morning. I got a pass and went down town for the first time[,] others have gone oftener, but perhaps it has saved me money to stay in camp.
Jan	7	The ground has been covered with snow for several days. The weather is not very cold. Iowa weather would stop nearly every kind of military effort. I think the rebs are pretty we[ll] crushed out, so far as real fighting is concerned.
Jan	8	Sergt. Foster, Neal, and Pencil arrived today looking fairly well.[19] We were made happy by home mail, enough to go around. As the boys stepped up to get their letters, their faces fairly beamed with happiness.
Jan	9	Today I visited the State Insane Hospt empty of course. The main building is old, and plain, but the wings are of recent construction, and as good as any similar building in the west[.] I would like to have a position in some such institution. Weather fine.
Jan	10	We had company drill this morning and again before going to parade. Men begin to show the effect of drills, and move with much steadiness. I

---

[18] The Eleventh's first chaplain was Rev. John S. Whittlesey (1812-1862), a Congregational minister from Durant, Iowa. He died 11 May 1862 of diphtheria (Iowa Adjutant General's Office, *Report of Brig.-Gen. Nathaniel B. Baker Adjutant General and Act'g Q.M.G....*, 2 vols. (Des Moines, 1867) 1:404; Charles Barney Whittelsey, *Genealogy of the Whittlesey-Whittelsey Family* [New York: Whittlesey House, 1941], 265-266).

[19] Sergeant Samuel Foster, James M. Neel and George Pencil. See Appendix B.

believe they will acquit themselves with honor. They are in good health now, Co. G has no one in the hospital, and turns out more men for duty than any other Co. The Col. seems to like our company.

Jan 11" Nothing worthy of note today, we drilled as usual.

Jan 12" A number went to church today, and it seems very quiet in the quarters. I put in my time writing to Grandfather. We have plenty of straw, and fixed up good beds[.] My health is good, weigh 160#

Jan 13" One of our Co. was courtmartialed today for sleeping on post, guarding rebel prisoners. I think they did it more to scare him. I am on guard today, weather quite cool, but we are very comfortable.

Jan 14 This morning Bledsoe was sentenced to three days hard labor.[20] Some of Co. G. who were caught running the guard got seven days labor and lost half months pay.

Jan 15 We had letters from home today. What a thrill of happiness comes to one on receipt of news from dear ones at home.

Jan 16" To day Capt. McFarland took about 25 down to a store to buy boots. We made a big hole in the visible supply, I paid $3.50 for a common pair. Some of the boys attacked small articles. The merchant did not complain.

---

[20] Benjamin H. Bledsoe. Presumably he is the soldier who was court-martialed the day before. See Appendix B.

Jan	17	To day while on guard I became sick and had to be relieved. A detachment of our Co. went into the country and took possession of Laramores farm[.] There is a fine house, completely furnished and full of good things, big piles of apples, plenty of turkeys, chickens, Horses, mules, buggies, carriages, wheat, hay, corn &c.
Jan	18	Some of the boys came in from Laramores[,] they forgot to bring us any of their good things. The place is worth about $60,000.[21] I am sick and have been for several days, dont improve much.
Jan	19	Regular Sunday inspection. A dull rainy, Sloppy raw day. Hard to find an item to jot down in my journal.
Jan	20	Ordered to march to Laramores farthest farm 16 miles from here. We spent the forenoon preparing, and after dinner started out at a 240 gait. All hands stood the march in good shape, and made the farm by dark.
Jan	21"	Boys are putting in the time breaking mules. It looked like a circus. The boys came off victorious and every mule had to take the oath.
Jan	22^d	On the road again for Fulton. We brought all the stock away with us, one rebel hog was executed and eaten.
Jan	23^d	At home again, rather lonesome only six of us, where there used to be thirteen and two sick out of

---

[21] In 1860 Henry Larrimore was valued in both personal and real property at $55,000. Will was pretty close to the mark (1860 U.S. census, Callaway County, Missouri, pop., sch., Dist. 18, Fulton p.o., p. 797, dwel. 119, fam. 122, Henry Larimore; NARA micro. publ. M653, roll 61).

this small number[.] received two letters, one from Merrill, one from Stilesville.[22]

Probably Will's uncle, Samuel Merrill Jessup (Courtesy of Jananne Slaughter)

Jan 25   I am to do hospital work tonight and tomorrow. We are living very well now, have plenty of fruit and vegetables.

Jan 26   I wanted to go to church today but cant get away from the hospital. Sunday is the great work day in the army. There is a rumor that we are to be attached to Gen. Lanes brigade we hope this is true.[23]

---

[22] Samuel Merrill Jessup (1833-1864) was Will's uncle. He later enlisted in Company F, Thirty-third Missouri Infantry on 22 August 1862. He was wounded in the left thigh at Tupelo, Mississippi 15 July 1864 and died six days later at the hospital in Memphis, Tennessee (Compiled service record, Samuel E. [*sic*] Jessup, Cpl., Co. F, 33 Missouri Inf.; Carded Records, Volunteer Organizations, Civil War; Records of the Adjutant General's Office, 1780s-1917, Record Group 94, National Archives, Washington, D.C.).

[23] James H. Lane (1814-1866) was a U. S. Senator from Kansas who was also a brigadier general of volunteers, commanding the Kansas Brigade in 1861. Another brigade command was proposed for him in December 1861, but the plan was later abandoned ("Obituary – James H. Lane, United States Senator from Kansas," *New York Times*, 4 July 1866, p. 5).

Jan 27 Early this morning while on duty in the hospital I heard several gun and revolver shots, but did not learn the cause until I came off. A Johnie had made a break and got away.

Jan 28" I got off from hospital duty yesterday almost sick myself. My lungs were sore and I had fever all day. I was afraid of Pneumonia. I put a wet pack on, and felt better.

Jan 31 On guard duty. Began a letter to Amelia and one to Grandfather. The weather is cold and cheerless.

Feb 1 This morning I came off guard and Lieut Lehew gave Walters and I a pass to the Laramore farm.[24] We started at once and started into have a good time. We had a fine dinner prepared by darky cooks, served in the dining room on a long table, brought a lot of apples back to the boys. I carried a sack into the pest house and gave the smallpox boys a lot.

Levi Jessup, Will's Grandfather (Courtesy of Jananne Slaughter)

---

[24] William F. Lehew and either Jacob Walter(s) or Rufus C. Walter. See Appendix B.

Feb	2ᵈ	Barr, Lowry, and Kauffman are sick, and I am not well.²⁵ This makes our duty rather heavy. Several of the boys talk of going into the gunboat service (Ellets River Battalion)[.]²⁶
Feb	3ᵈ	Were paid two months pay today. The Co. sent $17[.]40. home.
Feb	6	Last night was a rainy, cold night, I wrote Grandfather and sent $20. making 34 since I have been in the service.
Feb	7'	To day I went down town and bought a copy of the Spectator and a few other things.²⁷ In the evening I was detailed to hospital duty and was up from 8 to 3 am. I was told not to do any work, but my help was of no use so I had to do everything.
Feb	8"	To day was a cleaning up day, and all worked to polish up. I make it a rule to bathe and scrub every time I can get a chance. There is less card playing and more reading. At dress parade the news was read of the capture of Fort Henry. There were cheers and the firing of a salute.²⁸

---

[25] David H. Barr, brother to George W. Barr, Ambrose Lowry and Sergeant John W. Kauffman. See Appendix B.

[26] The Ram Fleet was raised by engineer Charles Ellet, Jr., initially under the direct control of Secretary of War Edwin M. Stanton. It later grew to include the Mississippi Marine Brigade. See Chester G. Hearn, *Ellet's Brigade: the Strangest Outfit of All* (Baton Rouge: Louisiana State University Press, 2000).

[27] Presumably the British weekly publication *The Spectator*, published since 1828.

[28] Fort Henry, on the Tennessee River, was taken on 6 February.

Feb	9	Sunday. On guard to day over the prisoners. Have a severe cold, which has been with me for two months, a good many have the same trouble.
Feb	10	There is more news about the evacuation of Fort Henry, which occurred on the 6". The gunboats drove them out. The boys hope to get into active service as soon as possible.
Feb	12	I had to go on hospital duty at 3 A.M. and worked hard until noon. The way I do the work, it is harder on me than guard duty. I think the work is valuable to me for future use.
Feb	13	I will be in the hospital again till noon. Dr Watson says I do the work better than any other man in the regt.[29] A brigade passed today. Cavalry, artillery and two regiments of Infantry. Yesterday the 5" Iowa, 47" Ills, 49 Ohio, with Artillery and cavalry.[30] With the two brigades were about 400 to 500 wagons.
Feb	14'	Am on guard today, at the guardhouse. We have quite a number of secesh prisoners, mostly from Price's Army. Between guard and hospital duty, I have had a little to[o] strenuous a time and feel it.

---

[29] William Watson (1826-1910), a native of England, was a prominent physician from Dubuque (*Report of Brig.-Gen. Nathaniel B. Baker Adjutant General*, 1:404; *Portrait and Biographical Record of Dubuque, Jones and Clayton Counties, Iowa* [Chicago: Chapman, 1894], 124-125; City of Chicago [Illinois] Department of Public Health death certificate no. 39262 [1910], William Watson).

[30] The Fifth Iowa and Forty-seventh Illinois were in the Department of Missouri at this time, but the Forty-ninth Ohio was part of the Army of the Ohio and was not in Will's vicinity until Shiloh.

Feb 15   To day I received a pass to go out to the farm, and see what rest and country air would do toward building me up a little.

Feb 16   To day is Sunday and it has been a restfull day[.] We read books, one of the boys plays on the piano and we sang old songs, ate apples and strolled over the large and beautiful farm. We went out scouting and found a lot of shot guns, rifles, and a cav. carbine hid out in trees.

Feb 17   Not far from the house to day I found a pretty small rifle in the creek, it had been thrown away during the skirmish at Overton run a few months before.[31]

Feb 18   We fired a salute for the great victory at Fort Donaldson [sic] Feb 16".[32] With several others I went hunting. We visited several houses, and talked with the men[.] Mr Davis talked very candidly, was a Southern rights man but thought the war could have been avoided. He invited us to come and eat dinner.

Feb 19   I returned to town feeling very much refreshed by my country vacation. The open country life, good

---

[31] The Battle of Overton Run took place 17 July 1861 about five miles south of Fulton between Missouri State Guard forces under Thomas B. Harris of Callaway County and Colonel John McNeil, Third U. S. Reserve Corps (U.S. War Department, *The War of the Rebellion: Official Records of the Union and Confederate Armies [OR]*, 128 vols. [Washington, D.C.: Government Printing Office, 1881-1901], [1], 3:401; *Journal of the Missouri State Convention...* [St. Louis: Missouri Democrat, 1865], 110-114; Carolyn Paul Branch, *Fulton, Missouri1820-1920: a History in Stories and Photographs* [Longbranch Press, 2010], 77-79).

[32] The surrender of both Fort Henry and Fort Donelson (on the Cumberland River) predicated the evacuation of Nashville by the Confederates and opened up West and Middle Tennessee to Union forces.

		food and plenty of fine fruit had a fine effect in restoring health.
Feb	20	On hospital duty again. They seem to like me for duty there. News came today that they had captured a thousand more prisoners at Fort Donaldson or vicinity. It was a great victory.
Feb	21	Off hospital duty. The weather is very fine here now. It is reported that Gen. Price has been severely handled by Gen Curtis' troops.[33]
Feb	22^d	The people of Fulton celebrated Washingtons birthday, firing a salute at sunrise and during the day there were addresses[.] There seems to be still some reverence for his memory.
Feb	23	There was a large delegation of the boys went to church today, more than fifty went this morning. I wished to go but I was invited to do hospital duty instead.
Feb	24	News came today that the rebels had evacuated Columbus.[34] It looks like the end of the rebellion is not far away.
Feb	25	We are all anxious to move south and get into active work, even if we have fighting every day.

---

[33] This was probably the Battle of Little Sugar Creek, Arkansas, 18 February 1862, part of the campaign which culminated in the Battle of Pea Ridge (*OR* (1), 8:559; see also William L. Shea and Earl J. Hess, *Pea Ridge: Civil War Campaign in the West* [Chapel Hill: University of North Carolina Press, 1992], 39-41).

[34] In Hickman County, Kentucky, Columbus was evacuated by Confederate General Leonidas Polk as a result of the Confederate defeats at Forts Henry and Donelson (*OR* (1), 7:436-437; "The evacuation of Columbus," *New York Times*, 1 March 1862).

		We have lost almost as many men since coming to Missouri as we would in a hard battle.
Mch	3^d	The guards were all removed to day and we have freedom to move around without so much red tape and passes.
Mch	4	Some of the boys are in from the farm making our room seem more cheerful tha[n] for some time back. Four of our Co are sick, myself among the number. Have been to[o] uncomfortable for four nights to sleep.
Mch	5	To day Co's D & F returned from Mexico where they had a rough time.[35] This evening we received orders to be ready to march soon, perhaps by Saturday, (8")[.] The news was hailed with joy, all anxious to get into active work. I am much better.
Mch	7	All the boys are in from the farm and our room is full. Our company is as full as any in the Battallion and shows up as well. The men are improved in condition.

---

[35] Company D arrived in the evening and took up quarters in the school room of the asylum. See Fultz Scrapbook, 7.

Chapter IV
"Bullits were zipping close to us"
The Road to Shiloh
March and April 1862

After the fall of Forts Henry and Donelson in February 1862, the Tennessee River was opened up for the southward advance of the Union forces. In order to man the thrust up the river, troops were collected from various locations. The Eleventh Iowa and other units that had spent the winter garrisoning northern Missouri were gathered into this movement. The two battalions of the Eleventh were reunited at St. Louis and were transported by steamboat down the Mississippi and up the Ohio and Tennessee rivers to Pittsburg Landing in Hardin County, Tennessee.

Mch	8	We marched for Jefferson City this morning, a trip of 25 miles. We reached the river opposite the city by evening and went into camp. After dark fires are burning in every direction groups of men are sitting around telling stories and singing songs.
Mch	9	A most beautiful sunny morning the birds are singing in the trees around, suggesting peace instead of war. We crossed the river boarded cars and about 2 P.M. started for St Louis
Mch	10	At 2 P.M. arrived in St Louis and went on board boat, bound down river.[1] Expected to pull out almost any time and did not hunt up any friends

---

[1] The Eleventh was transported by the *U.S.S Great Western*, which had been purchased by the War Department 10 February 1862 (Lurton Dunham Ingersoll, *Iowa and the Great Rebellion* [Philadelphia: Lippincott, 1866], 215; *Dictionary of American Naval Fighting Ships*, 8 vols. [Washington, D.C.: Government Printing Office, 1959-1981], 3:144).

		out at Camp Benton. Second battallion came during evening from California.[2]
Mch	11	Waked this morning to find the boat still at St Louis. Boat started about 8 A.M. and steamed slowly down the river. The regiment is large, in good condition and wants to do something. It will no doubt have a chance before long.
Mch	12	Traveling along at a fair rate. Passed Cape Girardeau about 10 A.M. Heard they were fighting below. Arrived at Cairo at 4 P.M. After a short delay started for Paducah, where we arrived before midnight and tied up.
Mch	13	Left Paducah this morning going up the Tennessee river toward Florence Alabama. Arrived at Fort Henry about dark. Found the 14" Iowa here. Saw one man I knew.
Mch	14	Steamed up the river all day, and at night reached Savannah, Gen C. F. Smiths headquarters.[3] Found here the 2^d-7"-10" Iowa, and many other regiments[4]

---

[2] See *Downing's Civil War Diary*, 36.

[3] General Charles Ferguson Smith (1807-1862) was commandant at West Point when Generals Grant and Sherman were cadets there. He commanded a division under Grant at Fort Donelson and was at this point commander of the army advancing up the Tennessee River. Injuring his leg, command reverted to General Grant (Warner, *Generals in Blue*, 455).

[4] The Second and Seventh Iowa were brigaded together under Colonel James M. Tuttle in General W.H.L Wallace's Second Division. The Tenth was at this time at New Madrid, Missouri. Will probably means the Twelfth Iowa, which was also in Tuttle's Brigade. See O. Edward Cunningham, *Shiloh and the Western Campaign of 1862* (New York: Savas Beatie, 2007), 238.

Mch	15	Are still on board the boat, about one hundred boats here. Said to be at least 10,000 men, with artillery and all kinds of equipage, and supplies.
Mch	16	We still remain on the boat. No one seems to know what we are going to do.
Mch	17	We will probably go ashore and camp before long. We are brigaded with the 8"-18" Ills and 13' Iowa with Dressers battery.[5]
Mch	18	This afternoon we began unloading our wagons and Commissary stores and will go into camp back of Savannah. We remained on the boat after working until midnight.
Mch	19	This morning we marched out to camp and after some delay we received our tents and soon had them up. It was nearly noon when we had breakfast. We were at once in the old life, drill and guard duty. We are comfortably fixed already.
Mch	20	Usual routine of camp life. We have been flooring our tents, making them home like[.] Living as well as if we had been here a year. It is rumored that we are to move[.]

---

[5] These regiments formed the First Brigade, under the command of the Eleventh's Colonel Hare, in Major General John A. McClernand's First Division of the newly named Army of the Tennessee under General Grant (Larry J. Daniel, *Shiloh: the Battle that Changed the Civil War* [New York: Touchstone, 1997], 319).

Jasper M. Dresser (1838-1894) was a Michigan born lawyer and merchant in Indiana and Illinois before going to Washington, D.C. in early 1861. He was one of the first volunteers of the war, being wounded at Bull Run. He was appointed chief of artillery on General McClernand's staff and was captain of a battery in McClernand's brigade (*Biographical Record and Portrait Album of Tippecanoe County, Indiana* [Chicago: Lewis, 1888], 366-369; "Died away from home – Col. Jasper M. Dresser, a Prominent Indianan, dies in Florida," *The* [Maysville, Ky.] *Evening Bulletin*, XIII:80, 26 February 1894).

Mch	21	Arose early this morning and after breakfast packed up ready to move, but it set in to rain and we put up our tents again, and settled down.
Mch	22	An appearance of leaving here. The 8" & 18 Ills and 13" Iowa marched down to the river this evening but we have no orders yet.
Mch	23	Began packing up early, and at 1 P.M. marched to the river and on board the boats.[6] Steamed up the river about 9 miles and went ashore about 3 P.M. Put up our tents near the landing (Pittsburg)
Mch	24	After breakfast broke camp, slung our knapsacks, and marched out two or three miles on the right hand road to Shiloh church. We camped with the rest of our brigade, in an old meadow full of sassafras.[7]
Mch	25	We had Battallion drill lasting till noon. I became very tired, there was so much double quick wheeling into line by companies. After dinner it was company drill. The weather is warming up.
Mch	26	Fine weather here now. The plum and peach trees are in bloom. Insect life abundant, also small reptiles. Troops are coming in all the time. A brigade or two are to leave soon, perhaps all will move.

---

[6] The steamboat *Westmoreland* (Fultz Scrapbook, 7).

[7] They were camped along the western edge of the Jones field (Shiloh Military Park Commission, *Map of Shiloh Battlefield, Positions on First Day, April 6, 1862* [1904]; *Downing's Civil War Diary*, 42).

Mch 27   Battallion and company drill to day[.] Our regiment is becoming quite proficient in the exercises.

Mch 28   The officers are putting us through as if the salvation of the country depended on it. Have four roll calls a day. Troops pour in all the time, all from Western states. I have found many friends among them.

Mch 29   We like our camp very much. There are some fine springs near and good water is abundant. Men bathe and take good care of themselves.

Mch 30   To day I made a long tour, visited the 2^d, 7", and 14" Iowa Regts.[8] Saw a lot of people I knew. Clark Hale was doing hospital duty, and had plenty to do.[9]

Mch 31   The men in our regiment look healthier than almost any other men here. I think because they are cleanly and take good care of themselves.

April 1   A most beautiful day. Weather very fine since we came here. There was much fun in camp over the tricks of some of the boys in selling out the rest with all kinds of Joshes.

---

[8] These regiments were all part of Gen. James M. Tuttle's First Brigade, Gen. W. H. L. Wallace's Second Division (Cunningham, *Shiloh and the Western Campaign of 1862*, 409).

[9] John Clark Hales (1838-1894), Company I, Fourteenth Iowa Infantry, an Ohio native from Mt. Pleasant, was living near Will's family in 1860 (*Roster and Record*, 2:814; 1860 U.S. census, Henry Co., Iowa, pop. sch., Jefferson twp., Marshall P.O., p. 1, dwel.5, fam. 5, Thos Ghaskill household; NARA micro. publ. M653, roll 324; Card records of headstones provided for deceased Union Civil War veterans, ca 1879-ca 1903 [NARA micro. publ. M1845], Records of the office of the Quartermaster General, Record Group 92).

April 3ᵈ   There was inspection review of the first division this morning. The sight was fine. Infantry, artillery and cavalry were all maneuvered[.] The battery fired a few rounds blanks.

April 4   Friday. I visited the 14" boys. While there at about 8 P.M. there was firing out front and much excitement. I went home and found the Brigade drawn up in line. We remained until 10 and then marched to quarters.[10] It was reported that the rebel army had been seen in front toward Corinth.

April 5   Saturday. We had a very spirited battallion drill this morning under Lieut. Col. Hall. Heretofore the men have not liked him very well, but to day he showed his efficiency so thoroughly that he gained greatly in favor.

April 6   Sunday. We were getting ready for inspection and had our guns to pieces cleaning them when Gen Rawlings rode through cam[p] shouting boys get your guns,[11] there had been firing out front for some time, but it was supposed to be pickets unloading their guns. It however grew heavier and just about this time about 7,30 or 8 A.M. a battery opened fire toward us the shots mostly passing high[.] The longroll beat and we got into line, where we remained for a time. We soon had

---

[10] The skirmishing that took place on this day was earlier in the afternoon (Cunningham, *Shiloh and the Western Campaign of 1862*, 129-133). The brigade was in line of battle for about four hours from 6 to 10 P.M. (Fultz Scrapbook, 8; *Downing's Civil War Diary*, 40).

[11] General John Aaron Rawlins (1831-1869) was assistant adjutant general on General Grant's staff and at that time a captain in rank. He later became President Grant's first Secretary of War. That Will Wade refers to him as "General" indicates that some editing may have gone on when he transcribed his wartime journals. Rawlins did not become a brigadier general until August 1863 (Warner, *Generals in Blue*, 391-392).

orders and marched a mile or more to the left (West) and formed a line.¹² We could see long lines of troops with flags marching toward us but could not make out who they were. Some of the men began firing, but were stopped as some of our men were in front of us. Bullits were zipping close to us and Wm Black fell dead.¹³ The firing became general. Dressers Battery began firing. After heavy firing for perhaps an hour the rebels poured around our right flank, and we were ordered to fall back, a good many were killed, and wounded, and so many Dressers battery horses were killed that only 3 or 4 guns were saved. Fell back perhaps 200 yards and formed a new lines among tents where cavalry had been camped. After an hour or more of fighting here we fell back again near a small ravine. At this place we got behind logs and trees and did good work. Theo Pallett was killed at this line.¹⁴ About this time we charged the rebels along with the 11" Ills and captured a flag. I got a piece about 6x8 inches square. Frank Hoe of Co B. was killed by my side.¹⁵ We kept falling back until evening when we reached the line of guns and partial breastworks planned by Col.

---

[12] The Eleventh's position was behind Dresser's battery and Water Oaks Pond (*Downing's Civil War Diary*, 40).

[13] William Black, see Appendix B.

[14] Theodore Pallet. See Appendix B.

[15] Corporal William F. Hough (1841-1862) was a native of Pennsylvania from Point Pleasant in Hardin County (*Report of Brig.-Gen. Nathaniel B. Baker Adjutant General*, 1:408; *Roster and Record*, 2:330; 1860 U.S. census, Hardin County, Iowa, pop. sch., Pleasant township, Point Pleasant post office, p. 706, dwel. 662, fam. 641, Jacob Hough; NARA micro. publ. M653, roll 323).

		Webster and held the rebels from any further advance.[16] Laid down on the ground, no bedding.
April	7	It began to rain in the night and we were hungry, wet, and miserable. There was little or no sleep. The gunboats fired heavy guns loaded with shells every few minutes all night. The roar and explosion of the shells was terrific. When morning came at last we got some breakfast[,] mostly crackers, and formed line again. We marched out near our old camps and acted as support to Buell's troops. There was some heavy fighting for about five or six hours, the rebels falling back all the time. By 4 P.M. the fighting was over and we went to our camp. Dead men and horses were in the company streets[.] The tents were shot full of holes and nearly every thing was gone or exchanged for old rebel equipage. We began to bury the dead, and estimate losses, our Company lost Wm Black, Mort Hobart[,][17] Theo Pallett, about 13 wounded. The regiment lost 41 killed, 225 wounded.
April	8	There was a false alarm, and we fell in and stood around without our breakfast for about two hours. Everybody was cross over the affair.
April	9	Still finding and burying the dead. We buried the rebels in long trenches, laying them in cross wise intil the trench was full, putting 150 to 200 in each

---

[16] General Joseph Dana Webster (1811-1876) was at that time a colonel and chief of General Grant's staff. On Grant's orders he placed a line of artillery on the bluff above Pittsburg Landing (Warner, *Generals in Blue*, 546-547; Cunningham, *Shiloh*, 305-306).

[17] Mortimer Hobert. See Appendix B.

trench. It is reported that 4000 were buried in this way.[18]

The Battle of Shiloh (Library of Congress)

April   10   Burial of rebels still going on. Many fell in out of the way places and were not readily found. Fire burned over part of the field toward the river burning many wounded, and disfiguring the dead.

April   12   Gen Halleck has taken personal command, bringing more troops.[19]

---

[18] Confederate casualties at Shiloh are reported at 1,728 killed. Will's figures for how many were buried in each trench would require about ten trenches. There were at least nine mass graves, the last of which contained 721 bodies. Only five burial trench locations are identified at Shiloh National Military Park. See Cunningham, *Shiloh*, 379-380, 422.

[19] Henry Wager Halleck (1815-1872), was promoted to major general on Winfield Scott's recommendation. He was at this time commander of the Department of the Mississippi, directing all operations in the Western theater. A

April	13	Sunday. A beautiful morning. Birds singing in the trees and wild flowers in bloom, Man the only maker of discord. Filling the fields with graves and hospitals with thousan[d]s of cripples[.]
April	15	A beautiful day. I am on hospital duty. It is six months today since we entered the service. Our regiment is much reduced turning out only 370 men.[20] Quite a number are sick[.]
April	16	Weather continues fine. Many are coming from Iowa and Ills and other western states looking after the dead and wounded.
April	18	Mrs Senator Harlan and her son visited the company.[21] Mr Dawson of Washington Ia and Chas McDowell of Mt Pleasant.[22]

---

better administrator than a field commander, he was for a time general in chief (Warner, *Generals in Blue*, 195-197; Cunningham, *Shiloh*, 88-89; see also Stephen E. Ambrose, *Halleck: Lincoln's Chief of Staff* [Baton Rouge: Louisiana State University Press, 1962], 39-46).

[20] According to Lieutenant Colonel Hall's report, there were 750 men and officers in the regiment on 6 April (*OR* (1), 10:130).

[21] Ann Eliza Peck married James Harlan in 1845, who was elected to the U.S. Senate in 1855. Their son William was born about 1853, but died about 1876. Their daughter Mary Harlan became the wife of Abraham Lincoln's son, Robert Todd Lincoln. Ann Eliza Harlan was one of the first prominent women to visit the sick and wounded at the front (Byers, *Iowa in War Times*, 455-456; *Portrait and Biographical Album of Henry County, Iowa* [Chicago: Acme, 1888], 620-621; 1870 U.S. census, Henry Co., Iowa, pop. sch., Center twp., Mt. Pleasant P.O., p. 225 (stamped), dwel. 1149, fam. 1110, James Harlan; NARA micro. publ. M593, roll 395).

[22] Probably James Dawson, a merchant of Washington, Iowa, who had a son in Company F, Lieutenant Josiah B. Dawson (*Report of Brig.-Gen. Nathaniel B. Baker Adjutant General*, 2:421; Charles C. Dawson, *A Collection of Family Records* [Albany, N.Y.: Munsell, 1874], 203-204; 1860 U.S. census, Washington Co., Iowa, pop. sch., Washington, p. 214, dwel. 504, fam. 484, James Dawson; NARA micro. publ. M653, roll 344).

April   19   A very cold rain is falling, and with leaky tents, and mud all around us are having a disagreeable time

---

Pennsylvania native Charles N. McDowell of Mt. Pleasant was a thirty-nine year old "speculator" in 1860 (1860 U.S. census, Henry Co., Iowa, pop. sch., Mt. Pleasant, p. 94, dwel. 412, fam. 406, C. N. McDowell; NARA micro. publ. M653, roll 324).

Chapter V
"Marched for Corinth"
Operations in Tennessee and Mississippi
April 1862 to January 1863

With General Halleck in command, the Union Army slowly advanced on the vital southern rail junction at Corinth, Mississippi. The principal engagements of this campaign were at Corinth and Iuka. The Eleventh spent much of the time at various locations on garrison duty.

April 25   To day we broke camp and marched out toward Corinth between two and three miles and pitched our tents. We were in a fortified camp.

April 26   General inspection to day by Gen Judah[.][1] It was very tiresome to me as I have had diarrhea for several weeks owing to the stench of dead men and horses, and poor water.

In the reorganization of the army after Shiloh, the Eleventh was brigaded with three other Iowa regiments – the Thirteenth, the Fifteenth, and the Sixteenth – under the command of Colonel Marcellus M. Crocker of the Thirteenth Iowa. This brigade dated from 27 April 1862 and remained together throughout the remainder of the war. It was known as Crocker's Iowa Brigade or simply the Iowa Brigade.[2]

---

[1] Henry Moses Judah (1821-1866) was inspector general of Grant's army at Shiloh, and later commanded a division under General Halleck (Warner, *Generals in Blue*, 255-256).

[2] *Downing's Civil War Diary*, 46; "Recollections of Crocker's Iowa Brigade," *Iowa Historical Record* v. 1, no. 3 (July 1885), 129-132; Stuart, *Iowa Colonels and Regiments*, 258).

April 27   After company inspection, we were all set to policing camp and improved its looks very much[.]

April 29   After being on guard all night I had to march, as our Division was ordered to Purdy.³ Marched through a swampy country till dark, then stacked arms in the woods and camped for the night.

April 30   After a pleasant night the Division had marching orders, and started for Purdy. Some two miles out we received different orders, and turned back to our camps again.

May 1   This morning we packed up and moved forward about three miles toward Corinth and about seven miles from the landing where we built a line of breastworks and went into camp. No enemy was encountered.

May 3   Camp No. 4.⁴ We broke camp and moved four or five miles toward the front. This morning there was a lively skirmish in which infantry and artillery both took part. It is reported our forces took a town.

---

³ Purdy was at that time the county seat of McNairy County, Tennessee. The Iowa Brigade was the Third Brigade in the Sixth Division under General Thomas J. McKean (Warner, *Generals in Blue*, 301).

⁴ Apparently the camps at this time were numbered, beginning with Camp No. 1 at Pittsburg Landing on 24 March 1862. Both Fultz and Downing use the same numbering. Camp 2 was established on 25 April and Camp 3 on 1 May. This pattern was maintained through Camp 9 at Corinth, established 6 June and where the regiment remained until 28 July (Fultz Scrapbook, 7, 9; *Downing's Civil War Diary* 46-47, 52, 60).

May	4	Sunday. A quiet day, raining much of the time. Our forces do not wish to push them on Sunday. It is rumored that the rebels are being reinforced.
May	5	The weather is clearing up, and it is a fine day.
May	6	News came that Yorktown had been evacuated by Gen Johnston.[5] I think this will make us more trouble than if McClellan had taken the place.
May	7	We are preparing to move more to the front.
May	10	Our whole regiment is on picket duty[.] The enemy seems to be very strong.
May	11	The Brigade had moved while we were on picket, and we marched off to hunt them. We soon found them, and were not long in fixing up again, Going to our camp we passed the Senior-Brigade.[6]
May	12	Camp No. 5.[7] Going through usual routine of camp duties. Drills and guard duty. A squad of absentees from drill, had to drill extra till night.

---

[5] Yorktown, Virginia was under siege from 5 April to the night of 3 May 1862 during McClellan's Peninsular campaign. See Stephen W. Sears, *To the Gates of Richmond: the Peninsular Campaign* (New York: Ticknor & Fields, 1992), 40-62. Downing also recorded the news (*Downing's Civil War Diary*, 48).

General Joseph Eggleston Johnston (1807-1891) was in command of what soon came to be known as the Army of Northern Virginia. Wounded in May 1862 at Seven Pines, he was replaced by General Robert E. Lee. Later that year Johnston was made commander of the Department of the West, defending Mississippi from the advances of Grant's forces (Warner, *Generals in Gray*, 161-162).

[6] This would have been the First Brigade of the Sixth Division, as the Eleventh Iowa was in the Third Brigade.

[7] Downing and Fultz both record Camp 5 as being established on 7 May (*Downing's Civil War Diary*, 48; Fultz MS, 22).

May	13	Camp No. 6.[8] We moved up about two miles to the front, and are quite near the enemy. They will have to show fight before long, or get out of this neck of the woods.
May	14	A very fine camping place is our present location.
May	17	There was quite a skirmish at Russels house, and the rebels were driven back.[9]
May	24	Camp No. 8.[10] The regiment is on picket duty today. We marched about two miles to some breastworks. The night passed without incident. We were on the alert quite early[.]
May	25	We were relieved during the forenoon and marched back to camp. The day is a beautiful one. A typical Sunday.
May	26	The day was quiet enough till toward evening when the batteries off to the left opened up and shelled the enemy in lively fashion. Keeping it up after dark.

---

[8] Again, according to Downing and Fultz, Camp 6 was established on 11 May and Camp 7 on 13 May (*Downing's Civil War Diary*, 48-49; Fultz Scrapbook, 10).

[9] The Confederates were driven by the Seventieth and Seventy-second Ohio Infantry regiments and Battery B, First Illinois Artillery under General James W. Denver and the First Brigade of Sherman's Fifth Division under the command of General Morgan L. Smith. The latter consisted of the Fifty-fifth Illinois, Eighth Missouri, and Fifty-fourth and Fifty-seventh Ohio. They were assisted by General Hurlbut's Brigade (report of Major General William T. Sherman 19 May 1862, *OR* (1), 10:1, 840; *The story of the Fifty-fifth Regiment Illinois Volunteer Infantry in the Civil War* 1861-1865 [Clinton, Mass.: Coulter, 1887], 138-142).

[10] Camp 8 had been established on 17 May (*Downing's Civil War Diary*, 49, Fultz MS, 22).

May	27	The batteries fired slowly much of the night, apparently feeling of the enemy. The engines whistled at all hours of the night in Corinth.
May	28	Battery firing from Gen Popes guns off to our left.[11] It looks like there would be a battle soon.
May	29	Some rifle firing off to the left front. Our line is being advanced. Gen. Pope is reported to be across the creek. Trains have been running and engines whistling day and night. Gen. Pope believes they are evacuating[.] From a treetop he could see into the town.
May	30	Early this morning there was a heavy explosion, and during the day Gen. Pope on the left, and Gen Sherman on the right advanced and found the rebel armies gone leaving their pickets to fall into our hands. Stores we set on fire and great piles of flour, meat, and forage were burning.
June	6	The Regiment moved out to Corinth. Several of the boys, and myself among the number were too sick to go, and we remained in the old camp.
June	7	Corinth, Miss. The regiment moved through Corinth and camped about a mile southwest of town. I was sick and it took me nearly all day to make the trip. The Regt. went on picket and left the sick to put up the tents.
June	8	The camp is very quiet as the Regt. is still on picket duty. Toward evening the[y] were relieved, and came in. Reported having a good time.

---

[11] General John Pope (1822-1892) commanded the Army of the Mississippi, the left wing of Halleck's forces, during the advance on Corinth (Warner, *Generals in Blue*, 376-377; Eicher, *The Longest Night*, 250).

June	11	I took a stroll to day hunting berries[.] I went south on the Mobile & Ohio track, saw about a hundred wagons, which the rebels tried to burn but failed in their hurry. I found few berries.
June	13	At noon our regiment went on picket about two miles from camp. There are no rebels near our lines anymore since they left and picket duty is a very innocent affair to what it was at one time.
June	14	I came on duty at 4 A.M. The crowing of chickens, and tinkling cowbells, and the silence of the wooded hills, carried me back to the old times of peace, and the quiet life of the farm.
June	15	Sunday inspection again. We are putting on the fancy touches again[.] Our brass shines like gold, and our leather fixings are shined to perfection.
June	16	Raining gently today. The[re] is nothing more refreshing than the brightness of the leaves, and the sweet odor that fills the air after a summer shower.
June	17	Regiment on picket duty again. Each Regiment takes the picket line for one day. So that we go on every fourth day.
June	18	About 1 A.M. I was on vidette duty under a big tree, and just about half asleep when a big owl over my head, let out his voice "Oo'hoo, oo hoo." I thought I was killed. Then about 4 A.M. I heard something approaching the post very cautiously, occasionally a twig would break, after a long time I heard the vidette north of me cry "halt" and the next came the loud bang of his gun, followed by a

squeal from an old sow! A loud laugh greeted the effort of the vidette.[12]

The Eleventh was in Corinth during the remainder of June and into July. The regiment was on picket duty, engaged somewhat in the building of fortifications and waiting for the local fruit to ripen. Colonel Hall, who had been wounded at Shiloh, returned to the regiment 29 June, bringing his wife with him.[13]

July	28	We broke camp to day and started for Bolivar, about 50 miles distant[.][14] Our guide misled us and we made poor progress. We found some fair peaches which tasted pretty good. At night we camped near Chewalla.[15]
July	29	Made an early start, and reached the Hatchie River about 3 P.M. Gen. Tuttle allowed the men time for a good swim.[16] Marched about four miles further and went into camp.
July	30	There was a light rain during the night. We got an early start and about noon crossed the M & C. R. R. at Middleton.[17] It rained some during the afternoon. We camped in an open field for the night.

---

[12] Vidette, or vedette, is the same as picket duty.

[13] *Downing's Civil War Diary*, 54-59.

[14] Bolivar is the seat of Hardeman County, Tennessee.

[15] Chewalla is in McNairy County, Tennessee.

[16] General James Madison Tuttle (1823-1892) was a brigade and division commander at Shiloh and was in command of the Sixth Division at this time (Warner, *Generals in Blue*, 513-514; *Downing's Civil War Diary*, 60; Fultz Scrapbook, 12).

[17] The Memphis & Charleston Railroad runs east and west through Middleton, in Hardeman County.

July   31   Continued the march toward Bolivar and after tramping 14 miles reached our destination and went into camp near the Hatchie river.

The Eleventh initially camped two miles east of Bolivar, Tennessee, moving across the Hatchie River on 14 August. The regiment was responsible for guarding a four mile stretch of the Mississippi Central Railroad.[18]

Aug   30   A brigade composed of the 2^d and 11" Ills Cav 9" Ind. Battery, 20"and 78 Ohio Inft. marched by to day and about five miles south west had a hard fight with the rebels under Gen Armstrong. Col Hogg of the 2^d Ills was killed. We could hear the artillery.[19]

Sept   1   We got news of the fight at Medon Sta about 18 miles north on the U & J. R. R.[20]
The 45" Ills, 7" Mo, and compan[y] of the 11" Iowa were in the fight. The boys made breastworks of cotton bales and all kinds of boxes and barrels, around the railroad station and gave the rebels a good whipping. Said to be Gen Armstrongs cavalry.[21]

---

[18] *Downing's Civil War Diary*, 61-65.

[19] Lieutenant Colonel Harvey Hogg of the Second Illinois Cavalry was a twenty-eight year old lawyer from Bloomington, Illinois (1860 U.S. census, McLean Co., Illinois, pop. sch., Bloomington, p. 538, dwel. 318, fam. 315, Harvey Hogg; NARA micro. publ. M653, roll 204).

[20] When Will Wade transcribed his original diaries he must have been unable to read the entry correctly. There is no U & J railroad. The location of Medon Station, between Jackson and Bolivar, indicates that it is the Mobile & Ohio Railroad (M. & O. R. R.).

[21] This engagement took place on 31 August 1862. Company H of the Eleventh was with a company from the Forty-fifth Illinois, about 150 soldiers. An account of the skirmish is in Phillip A. Hubbart, ed., *An Iowa Soldier Writes Home: the Civil War Letters of Union Private Daniel J. Parvin* (Durham, N. C.: Carolina Academic Press, 2011), 35-37.

The Eleventh remained in the vicinity of Bolivar, Tennessee, on guard as Fort Hall north of town was constructed and also guarding the railroad cut seven miles from town. The regiment left Bolivar on 12 September, and after spending a few days at Corinth, arrived in the vicinity of Iuka, Mississippi on 19 September.[22]

Sept 20   We arrived in Iuka too late to get into the fight. I walked over the battle field. The fighting was in thick brush and at close range. The 5" Iowa lost about 80 killed. I found the medicine chest of the 45" Alabama.[23] I carried it to our surgeon. Most of the troops were in pursuit of Gen Price.

Sept 27   Marched for Corinth where we arrived after a hard tramp, and camped South west of town.

The Eleventh remained in Iuka as garrison until 1 October when they left for Corinth, arriving 2 October.[24]

Oct 3^d About 8 A.M. skirmishing began on the Chewalla road and after a pretty stiff fight our forces had to fall back. By 10 the rebels made an attack on the west and northwest but were repulsed by heavy artillery fire from at least 40 heavy guns, and well directed rifle fire. They remained nearby all night and prepared for a new attack.

---

[22] *Downing's Civil War Diary*, 66-70; Fultz MS, 27-29.

[23] As Will states, the Eleventh was not involved in the Battle of Iuka, which took place on 19 September. Howevern the Sixteenth Iowa, of Crocker's Iowa Brigade, was engaged. The Forty-fifth Alabama Infantry was not present at Iuka. Will may mean the Thirty-seventh Alabama Infantry. See, Peter Cozzens, *The Darkest Days of the War: The Battles of Iuka and Corinth* (Chapel Hill: University of North Carolina Press, 1997), 82, 91, 106, 326.

[24] *Downing's Civil War Diary*, 70-72; Fultz MS, 29.

Oct   4   By daylight the rebels guns opened up and kept it up till about 9.30 they advanced along the Railroad and Bolivar road. The[y] struck Fort Powell and in spite of a terrific fire overran it and some of them pushed into the town. They were finally driven back. They formed and attacked Battery Robinette, but met such a heavy infantry fire, and crossfire from Batteries Phillips and Williams that they fell back. After a time they came on again led by Gen W. P. Rodgers and in the face of the most terrible fire ever seen they crossed the ditches and mounted the works, for a few minutes they had the guns, but they could not hold their position and fell back, leaving Gen Rodgers and 54 men lying in the ditch, Gen Rodgers horse, the regimental chaplain, A young boy not over fifteen was among them.[25] Later Van Dorn charged from the East but was repulsed.[26] This ended the battle.[27]

Oct   5   The retreating rebels were met by Gen Ords and Hurlbuts forces at Pocahontas and after a stiff fight drove them across the Hatchie River,

---

[25] Colonel William Peleg Rogers (1819-1862) of the Second Texas Infantry, was an attorney in Mississippi and Texas before the war. He had served under Jefferson Davis during the Mexican War. He was also a signer of the Texas ordinance of secession (*Handbook of Texas Online*; database, Texas State Historical Association [http://www.tshaonline.org/handbook : accessed 15 November 2010]; see also Daniel W. Barefoot, *Let Us Die Like Brave Men: Behind the Dying Words of Confederate Warriors* [2005], 56-61).

[26] Major General Earl Van Dorn (1820-1863) was at this time commanding the Army of Mississippi out of Vicksburg (Warner, *Generals in Gray*, 314-315).

[27] For the involvement of the Iowa Brigade at Iuka, see Cozzens, *The Darkest Days of the War*, 186-192.

capturing twelve guns, and killing about 500 of them.[28]

For the next few days the Eleventh pursued the retreating Rebel Army, reaching Ripley, Mississippi on 9 October. The regiment soon left for Corinth, arriving there the evening of 12 October, where it remained until 2 November. The next camp was at Grand Junction, Tennessee until 28 November. The Union Army was on the move south and the Eleventh moved on Holly Springs, Mississippi, driving the enemy along the way. They reached Waterford by 1 December and Abbeville on 3 December, where they remained for two weeks. After a brief push south to Oxford, Mississippi the troops returned to Holly Springs on 21 December. Nine days later the regiment marched north and arrived at Lafayette (now Rossville) in Fayette County, Tennessee 31 December 1862.[29]

1863

Jan 1   Lafayette Tenn. We are camped here to guard the M & C railroad.[30] Reb cavalry are very annoying trying all the time to cut the road. We have to be ready day and night for attack.

---

[28] This engagement took place at the Davis Bridge over the Hatchie River near Pocahontas in Hardeman County, Tennessee (Cozzens, *The Darkest Days of the War*, 280-290; see also Fultz MS, 32).

    Major General Edward Otho Cresap Ord (1818-1883) was wounded in this fight and was later commander of the XIII Corps at Vicksburg (Warner, *Generals in Blue*, 349-350).

    General Stephen Augustus Hurlbut (1815-1882) was Fourth Division commander in the Army of the Tennessee at this time and was later the XVI Corps commander (Warner, *Generals in Blue*, 244-245).

[29] *Downing's Civil War Diary*, 74-90; Fultz MS, 32-37.

[30] The Memphis & Charleston Railroad.

Jan 12 Struck tents and started for Memphis about 25 miles distant. Camped for the night about seven miles from the city.

Jan 13 Marched to within two miles of town and went into camp.

Jan 16 We were paid two months pay today.[31]

Jan 17 Went to theatre with some of the boys, was to meet Wade, but from some cause he was not there. Enjoyed the play, but when I went back through the snow to a cold tent I felt just a little bit discontented.

---

[31] Apparently 15 January was pay day (*Downing's Civil War Diary*, 94; Fultz MS, 38).

Chapter VI
"Mosquitoes more to be dreaded than rebs"
The Vicksburg Campaign
January to July 1863

General Grant had initially hoped to invade Mississippi through the central part of the state. But political considerations favored a move down the Mississippi River to capture Vicksburg, thus opening up the river completely to Union control and splitting the Confederacy in two. Thus the troops who had been maneuvering around northern Mississippi were gathered at Memphis and sent south along the river. General McArthur's division, which included the Eleventh Iowa, were sent to take part in the plan to connect lake Providence in Louisiana with the Mississippi River.[1]

Jan	18	We received marching orders again today, and packed up going on the boats towards evening. They were being loaded with army stores &c.
Jan	19	Boats loaded nearly all night and still at it. I went up town and had two ambrotypes taken. Sent one home, and kept one for uncle Jonathan.
Jan	20	We did not get away until 3 P.M. we ran down river about 30 miles and tied up on the Arkansas side.[2]
Jan	21"	Started again at daylight, and at noon reached Helena, where we laid up a while. I saw a lot of

---

[1] See Michael Ballard, *Vicksburg: the Campaign that Opened the Mississippi* (Chapel Hill: University of North Carolina Press, 2004), especially pp. 101-128, 173-174.

[2] The Eleventh was aboard the steamer *Maria Denning* with the Eighteenth Wisconsin, the Ninety-fifth Illinois and part of the Second Iowa Battery (*Downing's Civil War Diary*, 95; Fultz MS, 38).

		boys I knew but Jonathan was away. I left the picture with Americus Hales.³
Jan	22ᵈ	Steamed away at an early hour. Passed Napoleon at 10 A.M.⁴ Weather clear and cool. Rebs fired into Steamer St. Louis. No damage. Landed on Miss. shore about 9 P.M. Several houses were burning, making a fine illumination.
Jan	23ᵈ	Started about 5 A.M. and after running about 50 miles, tied up on Louisiana side, opposite mouth of the Yazoo river. The levee is lined with boats. It is only about six miles to Vicksburg.
Jan	24"	It is a rainy muddy day. I met Wade and we had a good time together.
Jan	25	Moved off the boats and fixed up camp[.] In the evening we pulled up and moved up the river about a mile and camped on the levee.
Jan	26"	I dug me a den in the levee, but it set in raining, and almost spoiled my place of abode.
Jan	27	It was a wet old night, but I am getting used to it. We would about as soon see a few rebs as so

---

[3] Hugh Byron Americus Hales (1842-1890), was brother to John Clark Hales and a member of Co. K, Fourth Iowa Cavalry, the same regiment as Will's uncle Jonathan Jessup (1850 U.S. census, Henry Co., Iowa, pop. sch., Jefferson twp., p. 213 [stamped], dwel. 758, fam. 758, Hugh Hales; NARA micro. publ. M432, roll 184; Hugh B. A. Hales, *Organization Index to Pension Files of Veterans who served between 1861 and 1900*).

[4] Napoleon was in Desha County, Arkansas, at the confluence of the Mississippi and Arkansas rivers. It was destroyed by floods in 1868 and 1874. See Mark Twain, *Life on the Mississippi* (New York: Harper & Row, 1965), 182-198.

much rain and mud. The 13" and 100 of the 11" are up the river on boats for a lot of wood.⁵

Probably Wade Matthews, Will's Cousin (Courtesy of Jananne Slaughter)

Jan 28 Moved up the river a mile and a half[.] Hummell and I built a shanty and McNeely and Heald came in and helped to fix it up.⁶ We built a chimney, put in shelves &c, all very comfortable. The ground was frozen last night.

Jan 29 Our boys returned at 10 P.M. yesterday[.] Col. Shane would not let them take meat, which they

---

⁵ Alex Downing of Company E was part of this detail. He claimed there were only 30 men from the Eleventh (*Downing's Civil War Diary*, 97).

⁶ William Hummell, William Heald and Sergeant George McNeeley. See Appendix B.

		found hid in a swamp[.]⁷ They were good and hungry.
Feb	1"	Millikens Bend. Raining and very disagreeable today.
Feb	2ᵈ	Heavy firing down at Vicksburg. Reported that the Queen of the West was running by the rebel batteries.⁸
Feb	3ᵈ	We have been trying to get service out of contrabands by having them do our cooking. Most of them are lazy, shiftless unless driven by the whip.
Feb	6"	Boys were out foraging, brought back some sweet potatoes. A good addition to our pork and cracker diet.
Feb	8"	Our Division is under marching orders.⁹ We packed up and boarded the boats re[a]dy to start up the river.¹⁰

---

[7] John Shane (1822-1899) was then lieutenant colonel, later colonel, of the Thirteenth Iowa (Stuart, *Iowa Colonels and Regiments*, 265-270; death notice, *National Tribune* [Washington, D.C.], 14 December 1899, p. 6, c. 5).

[8] A part of Ellet's ram fleet, the *Queen of the West* made a spectacular run past Vicksburg, ramming and sinking the Confederate *City of Vicksburg* on 2 February. It was captured later that month on the Red River (Hearn, *Ellet's Brigade*, 93-95, 105-107).

[9] The Eleventh was part of the Third Brigade, Sixth Division of the XVII Army Corps, then under the command of General John McArthur.

[10] The Eleventh boarded the *Empress* with the Tenth Ohio (*Downing's Civil War Diary*, 99; Fultz MS, 39).

Feb	9"	Got under way at 9 A.M. A fine sunny day, and the river beautiful. About dark we landed at Lake Providence about 45 miles above Vicksburg.
Feb	10	Left the boats and marched about two miles out to Gen. Sparrows plantation on the North bank of the lake.[11] We pitched our tents under the shade of evergreens a most beautiful camping place.
Feb	14"	Five hundred Negroes were brought in today and were put to work on the canal, which is a deep cut across the levee to let the Mississippi into Lake Providence and thence through the Tensas river to the Red River. The chief object being to flood the country and keep guerrillas away from the river.
Feb	16"	I procured a pass today and went to the camp of the 11" Ills Inft. to see Wade, but he was away and I did not get to see him.
Feb	19"	Company on picket today. Are having plenty of sweet potatoes and are having a better time than if in camp.
Feb	20"	Very pleasant weather. Mud drying up rapidly. Several hundred Negroes under the direction of Cap. Elrod are picking cotton on the abandoned

---

[11] Edward Sparrow (1810-1882), a native of Dublin, Ireland, was one of the richest men in Louisiana, his real and personal estate valued at $1,248,050 in 1860. Sparrow also served in the Confederate Senate (1860 U.S. census, Carroll Parish, Louisiana, pop. sch., Ward 2, Lake Providence post office, p.367, dwel. 463, fam. 452, Edward Sparrow; NARA micro. publ. M653, roll 409; Edward Sparrow petition, Case Files of Applications from Former Confederates for Presidential pardons ["Amnesty Papers"], 1865-1867; Records of the Adjutant General's Office, 1780's-1917, Record Group 94, National Archives, Washington, D.C.; see also, Jon L. Wakelyn, *Biographical Dictionary of the Confederacy* [Westport, Conn.: Greenwood, 1977], 397). Colonel Hall made his headquarters in the plantation house (*Downing's Civil War Diary*, 100).

		plantations near here.[12] They are paid 1.[00/100] per day[.] They seem to enjoy drawing wages like white men.
Feb	22[d]	Company inspection today, were lined up for vaccination.[13] We all wondered what our friends at home were doing to honor Washingtons birthday. Down here they dont seem to observe any kind of anniversary[.]
Feb	23[d]	We spend much of our time especially in the evening boating on the lake. The boats glide over the water to the accompaniment of musical voices. Many of the boys are making shell jewelry from shells found at Sparrows home place.
Feb	24"	Have to march again. We took blankets and three days rations and at 4 P.M. went aboard the Maria Denning, steamed for Greenville where guerillas had been firing into the boats lately[.][14]
Feb	25	Steamed away all night and at 8 A.M. arrived at Greenville. Gen Burbridges force had arrived first, a Brigade and two gunboats.[15] As all was quiet at 10 A.M. started back for camp which we reached at 5 P.M. A fine outing.

---

[12] Rev. John Elrod (1818-1889) was a Methodist minister from Washington County. He was first a captain of Company I, Thirteenth Iowa, then that regiment's chaplain (1860 U.S. census, Washington Co., Iowa, pop. sch., Cedar township, Wassonville post office, p. 38, dwel. 293, fam. 285, John Elrod; NARA micro. publ. M653, roll 344; John Elrod, *General Index to Pension Files 1861-1934*; NARA microfilm publication T288). Downing claimed it was only 100 Negroes picking cotton (*Downing's Civil War Diary*, 101).

[13] For smallpox (*Downing's Civil War Diary*, 101; Fultz MS, 40).

[14] Greenville is in Washington County, Mississippi.

[15] Stephen Gano Burbridge (1831-1894) commanded a brigade in the XIII Corps (Warner, *Generals in Blue*, 54-55).

USS Maria Denning (U.S. Naval Historical Center)

Feb	28"	Were mustered for pay this morning[.] Spent most of the day improving our quarters[.]
Mch	1st	Had both company and Regimental inspection today.
Mch	2d	The tents were inspected today, and nearly all were condemned. They all leaked like riddles. Ours was gum.
Mch	4	All hands getting ready for brigade inspection, which is to be very perfect.

Mch	[5]	Maj. Strong of Gen. McPhersons staff inspected us.[16] Afterward we signed two months payrolls.
Mch	6"	We were marched to a field about two miles away, and heard Adjutant Gen Thomas and other speakers, on the proposition to employ the negroes in every possible way.[17] Then the question was put to vote[;] it was one thunderous "aye."
Mch	7"	All but our mess got a soaking last night. Most of them were up all night.
Mch	8"	Just a year today since we left Fulton headed for Dixie and trouble. We had company inspection. Toward evening there was a hailstorm and it turned off quite cool.
Mch	9"	Annies Birthday. I have worked all day making her a shell ring, did not get it quite done.
Mch	10"	Am on picket again. Still working hard on Annies ring. Just as I had it almost complete I broke it, and felt much annoyed, as I had worked two entire days. I finished a small heart in shell.

---

[16] Major, later Lieutenant Colonel, William Emerson Strong (1840-1891), originally of the Second, then the Twelfth Wisconsin Infantry (William Ogden Wheeler, *The Ogden family in America* [1907], 302).

James Birdseye McPherson (1828-1864) was in command of the XVII Corps during the Vicksburg Campaign. The following year he commanded the Army of the Tennessee and was killed at Atlanta (Warner, *Generals in Blue*, 306-308).

[17] Lorenzo Thomas (1804-1875) was adjutant general of the army from 1861 to 1869. He had been sent to the Military Division of the Mississippi in 1863 to organize regiments of Black troops (Warner, *Generals in Blue*, 502-503). Fultz claims that the resolutions so unanimously approved concerned the condemnation of Copperhead activity in the north (Fultz MS, 40).

| Mch | 15" | We received two months pay today. I sent most of mine home by mail as this was the only way provided. |

| Mch | 16" | Turned over our old Sibley tents and drew new wedge tents. We kept our gum tent until we change camp. |

| Mch | 17 | They turned the water into the canal today. The roar was heard five miles. Were out on drill today, regular thing. |

| Mch | 21" | Our new Enfield Rifles were issued to us today. They are a much better as well as lighter arm than our old guns.[18] The water rose so that we had to move out. Marched three miles up river and camped in the mud. |

| Mch | 22^d | Fixed our tents up the best we could[.] Raised the sides about three feet and built two strong bunks. |

| March | 26" | Orders to march again. Packed up and went on board the Superior, just at dark.[19] Our destination is unknown to us. |

| Mch | 27 | We got off at daylight and went three miles below Lake Providence and camped on Websters plantation – a beautiful green place. We went for |

---

[18] The Eleventh Iowa had originally been issued old smoothbore muskets, probably Model 1840 flintlock Springfields, .69 caliber, that had been converted to percussion cap. Fultz described them as "old fashioned Harpers ferry musket pattern flint locks changed to percussion locks" ("History of Company D," 40; Cyril B. Upham. "Arms and Equipment for the Iowa Troops in the Civil War," *Iowa Journal of History and Politics*, v. 16 [1918], 22; *Downing's Civil War Diary*, 15).

[19] Downing also indicates they boarded the *Superior*, but Fultz has the *Empress* (*Downing's Civil War Diary*, 104; Fultz MS, 42).

the fencing[.] Col Abercrombie hol[d]ing his watch[,] in eight minutes they were gone.[20]

Lt. Colonel John C. Abercrombie (State Historical Society of Iowa)

April 1"   The entire camp participated in an observance of this time honored day. Some of the Jokes were a little rough but all observed good nature.

April 2ᵈ   Camp 3 (Websters). On picket, mosquitos more to be dreaded than rebs.

April 3ᵈ   Signed pay rolls for two months.

April 6   Just one year today since Shiloh. What memories come thronging the brain[.] The charge, the roar of guns, the shout of friends and enemies. The death of comrades. Most of it sad. war is awful.

---

[20] John C. Abercrombie (1823-), a dentist of Burlington, Des Moines County, was lieutenant colonel of the Eleventh. He had seen service in the Mexican War as a member of Company K, Fifteenth U. S. Infantry (*Portrait and Biographical Album of Des Moines County, Iowa* [Chicago: Acme Publishing, 1888], 256-257).

April 7"   A lot of sanitary goods were divided among the men today.[21]

April 8"   Adjutant Gen Thomas spoke to us today about arming negroes, and stated that there would be promotions of privates and Noncommissioned officers to positions as officers of negro regiments[.]

Adjutant General Thomas addressing the Negroes in Louisiana (Library of Congress)

---

[21] Evidently the gift of the people of Muscatine County, Iowa (Fultz MS, 43).

April 9" We received four months pay today. I sent 50.$^{00/100}$ home.

April 10" A Special muster of regiment to see how many recruits are needed to fill the ranks.

April 15 John Kauffman left for home discharged[.] Sam Foster received his commission as Second Lieut.

April 16 A swarm of bees settled near the camp[,] some of the boys found an empty keg and proceeded to hive them. Ritchie deserted.[.][22]

April 17 Gen review by Gen. McArthur.[23] At parade four promotions in our Co. One for me.[24]

---

[22] This may have been inserted into this entry at a later time as it appears to be squeezed in. Chester C. Richie of Company G was actually discharged 16 April 1862 at St. Louis. He later re-enlisted in Company M, Fourth Iowa Cavalry and served to the end of the war (*Roster and Record*, 377; Chester C. Richie, *Organization Index to Pension Files of Veterans who served between 1861 and 1900*).

[23] Brigadier General John McArthur (1826-1906), a native of Scotland, commanded the Sixth Division of McPherson's XVII Corps, to which the Eleventh belonged (Warner, *Generals in Blue*, 288-289).

[24] Will was promoted to corporal on this date, General Order No. 8 from Col. Hall (Compiled military service record, William L. Wade, Pvt., Co. G, 11 Ia. Inf., Civil War, RG 94, NA-Washington).

April	18	Another General review. We went through it with more credit.
April	19	Sunday[.] Also inspection. Never separate always arm in arm.
April	20"	Squad drill, which I rather like if you have a bright capable drill officer. Later we received marching orders.
April	21"	Lieut. Weir came from Iowa. We struck tents and boarded the Platte Valley in a drenching rain. Near night we steamed for Millikins Bend.[25]
April	22^d	At daylight arrived at the bend, and went into camp, near the levee.
April	23	All hands policing camp. I worked until my back ached.
April	24	On picket duty. In the night swarms of natives attacked us, on wings[.] There was much blood shed, but we held out until fresh troop[s] came.
April	26"	Turned over our tents, and at 2 P.M. we were on the road for below. Marched fifteen miles and camped near Richmond.[26]
April	27	Marched through Richmond and camped about a mile beyond, on account of rain. It took about $200. worth of cotton to make my bed that night.

---

[25] Milliken's Bend in Carroll Parish, Louisiana takes its name from the plantation of Richard M. Milliken, a sixty-eight year old native of South Carolina (1860 U.S. census, Carroll Parish, Louisiana, pop. sch., Floyd, p. 413, dwel. 893, fam. 865, Richard M Milliken; NARA micro. publ. M653, roll 409; Fultz MS, 45).

[26] Richmond is in Madison Parish, Louisiana.

April	28"	Marched at 8 A.M. traveled some eight miles through black mud and camped on Holmes plantation.[27] This is a fine place. The cotton gin is a fine and expensive building. The quarters for the slaves looked like an ordinary village of fairly good white frame houses.
April	29	The teams were sent back after rations[.] There is a tower on the gin house 80 feet high. The signal corps use it.
April	30	Heavy firing at, or below Vicksburg. We signed pay rolls for two months. Have had several good swims in the river lately.
May	1"	The weather is very pleasant here now. Lieut Weir is acting adjutant.
May	2^d	So many Iowa soldiers passing. The 4" 9" 26" and 31" went by today.[28]
May	3^d	The 8", 12", and 25 Iowa passed today.[29] They camped near us. I found a lot of acquaintances among them.

---

[27] The Trinidad Plantation in Madison Parish was owned by T.C. Holmes, a forty-eight year old native of Massachusetts (1860 U.S. census, Orleans Parish, La., pop. sch., New Orleans, p. 953, dwel. 2733, fam. 3007, T.C. Holmes; NARA micro. publ. M653, roll 420).

[28] The Fourth, Ninth and Twenty-sixth Iowa Infantry regiments were all at that time in the Third Brigade, First Division of the XV Corps, while the Thirty-first was in the Second Brigade.

[29] The Eighth and Twelfth were in the Third Brigade, Third Division of the XV Corps, having been transferred from the Department of Missouri. The Twenty-fifth was in the Second Brigade, First Division of the XV Corps.

May   5"   The 4" Iowa Cav. were going by today. Uncle Jonathan was with them. It was the first time I had seen him. He is Q[u]arter Master Sergt.[30]

Will's uncle, Jonathan Jessup (Editor's Collection)

May   6"   While we were drilling, 440 rebel prisoners marched about a quarter of a mile from us. They looked very forlorn.

May   7"   230 more prisoners went by today. Part of the same lot.

May   8"   Marching orders again. Will go in a day or two.

May   9"   Drilled twice today. More rebels passed in wagons, probably sick or wounded.

---

[30] Jonathan Jessup was promoted from private to Commissary Sergeant on 1 March 1863 (Compiled military service record, Jonathan Jessup, Pvt., Co. D, 4 Ia. Cav., Civil War, RG 94, NA-Washington).

May   10   Regimental inspection as usual today.

May   11"   Marched down river at 5 A.M. made 15 miles, camped five miles below New Carthage.[31] Near the latter place we passed the Tuscumbia tied up. She was all shot to pieces running the batteries April 16. She had 30 killed.

May   12"   Marched at daylight. Made about 15 miles, camped at Lake St. Joseph.[32] Saw some big alligators basking in the sun. Some had been shot.

May   13"   Started at 6 A.M. with two days rations, reached Hard Times Landing and crossed the river on the Chessman, to Grand Gulf[.][33] Were ordered to camp here a few days. I climbed up to the rebel earthworks, which well built and mounted five heavy guns[.] One had burst and killed several men among them the rebel chief of artillery Col Wade.[34]

May   14"   A guerrilla band stirred up some excitement. The[y] just dropped in to see if anyone was there. "We were."

---

[31] New Carthage, in Tensas Parish, Louisiana, was a supply base during the Vicksburg Campaign (see, Michael B. Ballard, *Vicksburg: The campaign that opened the Mississippi* [Chapel Hill: University of North Carolina Press, 2004], 192, 195).

[32] Lake St. Joseph is at Newellton in Tensas Parish.

[33] According to Fultz, this was the steamer *J. W. Chessman* (Fultz MS, 46).

[34] Captain William Wade was Confederate General John S. Bowen's chief of artillery at Grand Gulf where he was killed 29 April 1863 (Compiled military service record, William Wade, Capt., Wade's Battery, Mo. Light Artillery, Civil War, RG 94, NA-Washington; Ballard, *Vicksburg*, 217).

May	15	Two large gunboats passed up today. The Albatross and the Hartford. Admiral Porter came ashore in a boat and met Gen Grant and Gen McPherson.[35]
May	16"	Another gunboat today. The hills look so beautiful after being in a flat country.
May	17"	While the gunboat laid here the "Jackies" had a dance. The music was good, and they did it up in good style.
May	18	I went over to the 4" Iowa Cav to see the boys, and while there, the usual thing happened; the regiment marched out on a scout. They went about 15 miles and tore out some obstructions in Black River. Got back about dark.
May	19	After we were in bed, we had to turn out and go on board the boat, it took until about 11 P.M.[36]
May	20	About 10 A.M. arrived close to Vicksburg, a little too close in fact and had to back away. About 4 P.M. crossed to the lower end of the canal (Grants). Went ashore and marched to Young's Point[.] We boarded the Crescent City. I got a letter from Mother which I read and bunked down.
May	21	Off at daylight up the Yazoo river to Haines Bluffs. Lay around there a few hours, boarded the boat again ran down to the Point marched to the landing below, crossed to Warrenton marched up

---

[35] As acting rear admiral, David Dixon Porter (1813-1891) was in command of the Mississippi River Squadron during the Vicksburg Campaign (James Russell Soley, *Admiral Porter* [New York: Appleton, 1903], 245, 312-349).

[36] The steamboat was the *Forest Queen* (Fultz MS, 47).

river about three miles.[37] The darkies poured out to the roadside as we marched, bringing water and little offerings, thanking the Lord that deliverance had come. We laid on our arm[s] all night.

May 22   Fell in at daylight, and marched about six miles, driving the rebel pickets in and were shelled in return, no one hurt. Our Co was deployed, and soon got into a hot place, in trying to work up nearer their works. Shells burst over, and all around us, there were some narrow escapes. We were close up to heavy forts. Gen McArthur and Col. Abercrombie walked out in front to a gate post in a field and used their glasses. They returned, sent a report to Gen Grant, and Gen. McClernand was relieved of his command.[38] After dark we melted out, and the regiment marched 5 miles N.E. and laid down tired, dirty, hungry.

May 23^d Marched to the left of Gen Smiths division and rested till 12 [P.]M. then returned to our position on the left, bringing a battery of light guns with us.[39]

May 24"   Regiment on picket today. Were shelled but no one was hurt, we laid low and let them shell away.

---

[37] Warrenton is in Warren County, Mississippi, about five miles below Vicksburg.

[38] Will must have subsequently edited this entry as General John Alexander McClernand (1812-1890), a politically appointed general and apparently Grant's nemesis, was not relieved of command of the XIII Corps until 18 June 1863. Neither General McArthur nor Colonel Abercrombie had anything to do with McClernand's dismissal (*OR*, 24 [1], 164-165; Warner, *Generals in Blue*, 293-294; Ballard, *Vicksburg*, 359).

[39] General Andrew Jackson Smith (1815-1897) at this time commanded the Tenth Division in McClernand's XIII Corps (Warner, *Generals in Blue*, 454).

		Our battery did no good, it was too light. At dark the 15" Iowa relieved us and we moved back.
May	25"	We are in reserve today. Gen Laumans division relieved us.[40] I took a good bath between acts.
May	26"	At 10 P.M. there was an alarm and we fell in and laid on arms all night. This forenoon marched to Gen McPhersons Headquarters and received orders to march to Black River tomorrow morning.
May	27"	We were off at daylight, marched about 20 miles, over hot dusty road, saw Jonathan and other boys of the 4" Cav.
May	28	Marched at 2 P.M. Made ten miles during the afternoon, it was a good hot one.
May	29	Off at 6 A.M. arrived at Mechanicsburg at 11 A.M.[41] Came up with rebels skirmishing with the cavalry. They soon broke away. Several men of cavalry wounded.[42] We were in the advance near a house where there was plenty of sugar and honey. It filled a long felt wan[t]. I had a little too much, and did not feel so well.

---

[40] General Jacob Gartner Lauman (1813-1867) commanded the Fourth Division of the XVI Corps. He was relieved of command after his troops were badly cut up at Jackson, Mississippi on 12 July 1863 (Warner, *Generals in Blue*, 275-276). The Eleventh was relieved by the Forty-sixth Illinois (Fultz MS, 49).

[41] Mechanicsburg is an area in Yazoo County, northeast of Vicksburg and southwest of Yazoo City.

[42] Major Alonzo B. Parkell of the Fourth Iowa Cavalry "succeeded in driving the enemy, with the loss of one officer and six men wounded" (William Forse Scott, *The Story of a Cavalry Regiment: The Career of the Fourth Iowa Veteran Volunteers* [New York: Putnam, 1893], 99). See also, *OR* I:24 (2), 302.

May	30"	Marched at 5 A.M. west along the Yazoo bottom. We destroyed everything as we went. Set fire to a fine gin, and $50,000. worth of cotton (1.10 per lb).
May	31	Got away at 6 A.M. and after a hot march of 15 miles reached Haines Bluffs. The reb cavalry followed at our heels all the way, skirmishing with the 4" Iowa Cav.
June	1"	Received letters from Amelia and Wade. We are out of rations and the boys are yelling "Crackers," "Sowbelly" loud enough to raise the dead.
June	2^d	We drew new clothes today. The siege goes on at a lively rate, Mortar shells dropping constantly. at night we can trace them all the way by a little streak of fire, then a heavy dull roar, and the earth trembles.
June	3^d	Drew three days rations today, and received orders to march tomorrow.
June	4"	Marched for Vicksburg, ten miles away, at 5 A.M. Went into camp near our 2^d Brigade.[43]
June	5	Gov. Kirkwood and Adjt. Gen. Baker spoke to the Brigade today.[44] They spoke in terms of high

---

[43] The Second Brigade of McArthur's Sixth Division was commanded by Gen. Thomas E. G. Ransom and consisted of the Eleventh, Seventy-Second and Ninety-fifth Illinois, and the Fourteenth and Seventeenth Wisconsin infantry regiments. Will's cousin Wade Matthews was in the Eleventh Illinois (James R. Arnold, *Grant Wins the War: Decision at Vicksburg* [New York: John Wiley, 1997], 324).

[44] Samuel Jordan Kirkwood (1813-1894) was the Republican governor of Iowa from 1860 to 1864 (*Portrait and Biographical Album of Henry County, Iowa*, 127-128; see also Dan Elbert Clark, *Samuel Jordan Kirkwood* [Iowa City: State Historical Society of Iowa, 1917]).

appreciation of what Iowa soldiers had done on every battlefield from Wilsons Creek to Vicksburg.

June 6   Weather quite warm today. Spent the day fixing up more comfortable.

June 7"   The boys left at Grand Gulf came today bringing our knapsacks and camp stuff. Had company inspection.

June 8"   Boys are lying around in the shade, doing very little, but dusting and polishing things up. I put all my impediments in order.

June 9"   The celebrated "Lottery" came off today[.] Thirty, or forty bright, intelligent girls back in Iowa were put into a lottery and drawn by as many brave young men! That is their names were placed in a hat, and we drew out one name each, agreeing to write to the aforesaid young lady. I drew the name A.E.C.

June 10"   A fine refreshing [rain] fell today, laying the dust, and purifying the air. We are camped in a cane brake about 25 feet high and thick as grass.

June 11"   Troops from all parts of the west are arriving here, and things are settling down for a regular siege.

June 12"   We moved our camp about a mile t[o]ward the rear, and close by Brigade Headquarters.

Nathaniel Bradley Baker (1818-1876) was Iowa's state adjutant general after having been governor of New Hampshire in 1854-1855 (Stuart, *Iowa Colonels*, 16-21; Johnson Brigham, *Iowa: Its History and Its Foremost Citizens* [Chicago: Clarke, 1918], 338-341).

| June | 13" | Had just got fixed up in good shape, when we were ordered on a four days picket. Marched about four miles to the rear where Co. "G" took an advanced position, found plenty of blackberries and plums. I had all I could eat of both. |

| June | 14" | Moved back a mile, and fixed ourselves more comfortable. |

| June | 15 | Having a great time cooking and eating blackberries. They are fine as silk[.] Jule Schreiner went to Pioneer Corps.[45] |

| June | 16 | It rained a fine shower today, laying the dust. Several of the boys are sick doubling up duty on the well ones. I am feeling fairly well myself. |

| June | 17 | Drew clothing today, and went on picket duty. Very quiet on our line. |

| June | 18 | The weather is all that could be asked. |

| June | 19" | Our chaplain returned to us. He manages to preach about two sermons a year.[46] |

---

[45] Charles Julius Schreiner. See Appendix B. Pioneers were skilled soldiers used to clear roads and build bridges and fortifications, much in the manner as engineer companies. Beginning in late 1862 they were often organized into companies and collectively known as the Pioneer Corps or Pioneer Brigade (Garrison, *Civil War Usage*, 192; see also , for example, *OR* 17 (2), 492).

[46] The Eleventh's second, and last, chaplain was Rev. Chauncey H. Remington (1827-), a Baptist minister appointed 25 June 1862. He resigned 7 August 1863. Downing also remarked on the chaplain's absence (*Roster and Record*, 285; 1860 U.S. census, Muscatine Co., Iowa, pop. sch., Muscatine, p. 824, dwel. 1396, fam. 1351, C. H. Remington; NARA micro. publ. M653, roll 337; *Downing's Civil War Diary*, 105, 123).

June	20"	The forts and naval force opened on the city at 4 A.M. and kept at it until 10 A.M. The roar was incessant[,] the earth shook like an earthquake.
June	21"	On picket today. Chaplain preached to balance of them.[47]
June	22^d	Orders to be ready to march at a moments notice.
June	23^d	Fell in and marched out at 6 A.M. Joined the Brigade and laid by till 11 A.M. then as soon as it was good and hot, we got off. Marched 8 or 10 miles and at 5 P.M. camped. It began to rain gently. I got overheated during the day.
June	24"	It rained all night. The firing on the city is heavy this evening. Deserters say most of the people live in caves dug in the hillsides and that provisions are very scarce and dear.
June	25	Still lying around under the trees wa[i]ting to be told what to do.
June	26	Ordered to get ready and march this evening. Later told to wait until morning. We are near some beautiful springs of water.
June	27"	Marched at 5 A.M. took a southern direction for six miles and camped on the road which crosses Black River at Messingers Ferry. Co. G went on picket duty.
June	28"	Relieved of picket duty, captured seven sheep who refused to take the oath, along with other animals. Chaplain preached in the morning on swearing.

---

[47] The text was John 14:2 (*Downing's Civil War Diary*, 123).

| June | 29 | Company went out to Messingers to day, while I was a short distance away, at night they came back with all kinds of plunder mirrors, books, clothes &c.[48] |

| June | 30 | Mustered for pay. We are behind four months. We have been on the fly so much of the time, that it was not safe to follow us. |

| July | 1" | The weather is very hot just now. Winder and Flory returned from hospital today.[49] The boys are betting on the fall of Vicksburg as we know that things are approaching an acute condition in there. Their guns are kept silent by our sharpshooters. Food scarce and bad in quality. And those terrible shells bursting in every nook and corner, make life unbearable. |

| July | 2^d | Absolutely quiet here, as much so as if there was no war. |

| July | 3^d | We were called into line at 9 P.M. and marched out to Messingers Ford, and laid in line to keep Johnstons troops from going to the relief of Pemberton[.] |

| July | 4" | We celebrated the day by shelling some rebel cavalry across the river. We did it all ourselves. The news came of the surrender of Vicksburg. Very little demonstration was made over the |

---

[48] George Messenger was a wealthy farmer of Warren County, his real and personal estate being valued at over $200,000 in 1860 (1860 U.S. census, Warren County, Mississippi, population schedule, Vicksburg post office, p. 1058, dwelling 1351, family 1327, Geo Messenger; NARA microfilm publication M653, roll 592).

[49] Thomas C. Winder and Francis M. Flory. See Appendix B.

		matter. No one seems to fully realize the truth of the report.[50]
July	5"	We were retired by Gen Tuttles Brigade, and marched back to camp. Whiskey was found in some way, and very soon the camp resembled a mad house. I got off by myself and wrote a letter to Amelia.
July	6"	Went on Picket, but were relieved at noon, and returned to camp, to get paid off. I received 35.$^{12/100}$. I sent $12. to New York for gold pens.
July	7"	Some prisoners passed in today, captured near Big Black. We went on picket again. Came across some fine green corn and had a feast.
July	8"	It rained last night like "Noah's flood." I received a good wetting but did not make any fuss about it. Relieved from picket duty.
July	9"	There is a great deal of gambling going on since payday, some men losing all their pay.
July	10"	Nothing much to record today. Hummell and I study Phonography a part of each day.[51]

---

[50] Fultz indicates that was because the news was announced by Colonel Chambers, the brigade commander, who was particularly unpopular with the troops (Fultz MS. 55).

[51] "Phonography" usually refers to the shorthand developed by Isaac Pitman about 1837.

Chapter VII
"Plenty of peaches and green corn"
The March to Jackson
July 1863

After the surrender of Vicksburg, General Grant turned his attention to Confederate forces under General Joseph E. Johnston at the Big Black River. Grant sent General Sherman with three army corps after Johnston, who retreated to Jackson. Sherman laid siege to the Confederates there and on 16 July, Johnston withdrew.[1]

July 11" Started quite early to escort a supply train going out to Jackson.[2] Rode in the wagon part of the time.

July 12 It was midnight when we arrived at Clinton 25 miles from Big Black river.[3] Marched today to within 3 miles of Jackson, about 9 miles. Heard news of surrender of Port Hudson to Gen Banks Army.[4]

July 13" Marched at daylight for Big Black. Toward evening passed the Brigade coming out. Also thousands of Paroled Prisoners, some of them fine

---

[1] Ballard, *Vicksburg*, 404-409.

[2] The supply train consisted of 245-250 wagons carrying provisions and ammunition for Sherman's troops (*Downing's Civil War Diary*, 128; Fultz MS, 57).

[3] Clinton is in Hinds County, Mississippi.

[4] Realizing his position was untenable after the fall of Vicksburg, Confederate General Franklin Gardner surrendered Port Hudson to Union General Nathaniel Banks on 9 July 1863, placing the Mississippi River completely in Federal control (Ballard, *Vicksburg*, 410-411).

		looking soldiers. They had had a hard time and nearly all declared they had enough of it. Arrived in camp 5 P.M.
July	14	We are resting after our trip. The teams are loading again. We are to act as escort.
July	15"	In the morning I wrote to Amelia. At 4 P.M. we started back for Jackson. Reached Edwards Station and camped.[5] Company went out on picket.
July	16"	The train came up to us at 6 A.M. and we moved on two men to each wagon, when within about 9 miles of Clinton, there was a false alarm. A Herald correspondent took the back track, arrived at Clinton at 4 P.M. found the Brigade and went into camp.
July	17"	Spent most of the day at Clinton, fixed up a wickiup. We heard that Jackson was evacuated.
July	18"	We are resting and living very well on plenty of peaches and green corn. We were needing these things to preserve health.
July	19"	Weather very pleasant. I walked over to a house not far away, which the family had left suddenly. It contained good furniture, two pianos, a melodeon, a good library. All were torn and smashed to pieces. War is playing havoc in the South. I saw paroled prisoners from Port Hudson, they had walked 150 miles to reach their homes.
July	20	Last night after most of us were in bed we had to get up and relieve the 16" from picket. They had

---

[5] Also known as Edwards Depot, it is located in Hinds County.

		to go as train guard. Were relieved this morning, we moved a short distance and fixed up better.
July	21"	Started for Black River, found the marching very hot and dusty, are taking back about 600 prisoners from Jackson. I came very near to giving out, we have had a hard lot to stand up against.
July	22	Marched toward Big Black, made 10 miles and camped for the afternoon and night near a corn field.
July	23ᵈ	Were up and off at 4.30 A.M. reached the river about noon, went on three miles farther making 18 during the day. Camped for the night. It is about 8 miles to Vicksburg. It was very hot and dusty. A good many gave out. The 13" Corps is passing.
July	24"	I was out on a hunt for peaches, found very few. Had a good sweat and little else. Had a good letter from Mother yesterday, answered it today. Wrote to Grandfather and Merrill.

Will's Mother, Emily Snoddy (Courtesy of Vance Gustafson)

July	25"	Moved camp at 4 A.M. before having any breakfast[.] Marched three miles nearer the bridge, camped close to railroad, on hilly ground

		covered with beech, elm & oak trees. Water is plenty and of good quality. It is a beautiful camp.
July	26	Inspection at 8 A.M. About noon Jay Miller while walking in the woods found Corporal Jas McGavic lying dead under a tree. He had walked out from the hospital a few minutes before.[6]
July	27"	A light rain fell during the night. I am on camp guard. Orders came to move to Vicksburg. We packed up, and started at 4 P.M. five miles from the city we camped for the night, near the railroad.

---

[6] Madison J. Miller and James McGavic. See Appendix B.

Chapter VIII
"We are taking our ease"
In camp at Vicksburg
July and August 1863

Will and the Eleventh spent the next month in camp near Vicksburg, spending time relaxing, on guard and picket duty, and drilling occasionally.

July	28"	Took up our march at 5 A.M. and at 8 reached the outskirts of the city, seeing for the first time what we had labored and fought so long to win. We saw in the hillsides the caves, which the citizens had dug to shelter themselves from the shells. The buildings were many of them badly damaged, and a few almost destroyed. We went into camp on the North side, outside the lines.
July	29	Spent most of the day sightseeing. I secured some pieces of the Pemberton tree, under which, it was said that the Surrender took place, about halfway between the lines. I also got a copy of the Vicksburg Citizen printed on wallpaper. Visited the water battery of heavy guns at the North side (up river) which was so destructive to the boats running by the batteries, and later to the Cincinnati[.] Went swimming and had a fine time.
July	30	A beautiful morning. Spent the day building a shebang and a bunk.[1] Made myself very comfortable. Wrote to Robert and sent him $5. Stubbs, Hudson and Woodworth are to go home on furlough.[2]

---

[1] A "shebang" is a temporary shelter (Garrison, *Civil War Usage*, 225).

[2] Martin D. Stubbs, Andrew J. Hudson and either Omri Woodworth or John B. Woodworth, brothers. See Appendix B.

July	31	Weather continues to be fine. Nothing worthy of record.
Aug	1"	It rained to day[.] I was not well fixed and my household stuff got a good soaking.
Aug	2^d	Had a fine swim in the river. Stubbs, Hudson and Woodworth started home[.] I sent a letter and books to Amelia by Mart Stubbs.
Aug	3^d	Our tents came last evening and today we fixed them up. We raised ours up, put in bunks and made a very comfortable place of it.
Aug	4"	Spent most of the day completing the improvements of our tent. Jas Richardson returned to company after almost a years absence.[3] I received some papers.
Aug	5"	Wrote letters to Uncle Solon, Amelia, and Johnson & Co New York. The weather is hot and oppressive. I tried a shower bath.

Will's uncle, Solon R. Jessup (Courtesy of Vance Gustafson)

---

[3] James Richardson. See Appendix B.

Aug 6"   We have had no other bread for a year but hardtack, today they brought out a portable oven from the city and we will have fresh bread. We were paid for two months today by Maj. Stanton.[4]

Aug 7"   To day we are taking our ease, after a rather strenuous campaign.

Aug 8"   Drilled from 7 to 9 A.M. Afterward started out to find Cousin Wade. After a long round found him within 3/4 of a mile of starting. He was sick, and somewhat discouraged. I remained all afternoon. Parade time when I reached home. Frank Flory my bunky had made some extra money, and bought 2 dozen cans of oysters. I did the cooky act.

Aug 9"   Preparing for inspection. Wrote to Mother[,] sent $15. Had a letter from Wade.

Aug 10"   Nothing worthy of note today.

Aug 11"   On camp guard duty today.

Aug 12"   My gold pens came from New York. I sold one to Foster and one to Sharp.[5] Sent $2.50 for six penholders.

Aug 13   After drill I procured a pass and went to see Wade, he was about well again. I also visited the Corps Hospital, saw Courtney, Beeler, Wooley

---

[4] Thaddeus H. Stanton (1835-1900) was the army paymaster. He remained in the army after the war and became known as the "Fighting Paymaster" (Gue, *History of Iowa*, 4:250; death notice, *Omaha Daily Bee*, 27 January 1900, p. 2, c. 2).

[5] Robert J. Sharp. See Appendix B.

		and Kendall.[6] After a good dinner with them I started for camp, it began raining and I was thoroughly soaked.
Aug	14	Rufus Walters who has been quite sick at the hospital is worse, and it is said will hardly recover.
Aug	15"	Rufus died this morning about 8 A.M. He was a lovely character and all the boys liked him. Wade came to see me, after dinner he did not fell well, and had to go home. Rufus was buried this afternoon. The services were very affecting.[7]
Aug	16"	Regimental inspection. Co. G looked their best. Joe Yeager went home on sick furlough.[8]
Aug	17"	Two days ago the boys made some "beer" and today we tried some of it. It knocked me out the first round.
Aug	18"	Were on picket not far from camp. During the afternoon we had a heavy storm of rain and wind, with severe lightning, it was risky to be out in it. Had a letter from Amelia and Grandfather.
Aug	[19]	My night was not very agreeable, when off post, I had a wet gumblanket, and water soaked earth swept by the wind to lie on. My rheumatism kept me from sleeping, if a million mosquitoes did not. Wrote to Amelia, Grandfather and Mother[,] sent her $10.

---

[6] Joseph L. Courtney, John Beeler, David Wooley and Jesse Kendell. See Appendix B.

[7] Rufus C. Walter died of dysentery. See Appendix B.

[8] Joseph Yeager. See Appendix B.

Chapter IX
"Our company is pretty well played out"
Shreveport March
August and September 1863

What Will refers to as the "Shreveport March" was an expedition to Monroe, Louisiana whose objective was an enemy encampment there and also to quell guerrilla activity in the area. The expedition was commanded by Brigadier General John Dunlap Stevenson (1821-1897) and consisted of troops from the XVII Army Corps, including the Eleventh. The expedition embarked on 20 rather than 21 August as Will records it.[1]

Aug 20" Have orders to march in the morning with blankets only. Received a letter from Mother and Annie dated Aug 2^d.

Aug 21" Marched down to the boat, and laid around till night.[2] I was on guard duty aboard the boat. Our company is pretty well played out.

Aug 22^d Arrived at Goodrichs Landing at daylight[.][3] Marched out about four miles and camped for the night. A lot of yams looked good to the boys. We proceeded to swear them in.

Aug 23^d We marched back nearly to the landing[.] Did not start until it was hot. Made about 10 miles camped near the Tensas.

---

[1] Report of General Stevenson, *OR* 26.1, p.248-249; Fultz ms., 61-63. See also John D. Winters, *The Civil War in Louisiana* (Baton Rouge: Louisiana State University Press, 1963), 301-302; Warner, *Generals in Blue*, 476-477.

[2] Fultz identifies the steamboat as the *Fanny Bullet*, while Downing refers to it as the *Fanny Bell* (Fultz MS, 61; *Downing's Civil War Diary*, 136).

[3] Goodrich's Landing is located in East Carroll Parish, Louisiana.

Aug	24"	Were all ready at an early hour, but did not move until it grew hot. Marched about 6 miles, and camped on Tensas river[.] The country here is slightly undulating and looks more civilized. The cavalry had a skirmish near here. Up to this point the country had been overflowed and smelled like a stagnant pond.
Aug	25"	Left the Tensas River at 7 A.M. After marching 12 miles we camped near a bayou for the night.
Aug	26"	Marched away at 6 A.M. Crossed the Boe[u]f River about noon. Made about 12 miles during the day.
Aug	27"	We[re] on the road early, our Brigade taking the advance, marched about 12 miles and halted for dinner. About 12 M. resumed our march through pine barrens, after 8 miles more we stopped near a stream for the night.
Aug	28"	Did not start early as it was only 8 miles to Monroe.[4] When we did march it was quite warm. When within 1 ½ miles of Monroe we learned that rebs had levanted, leaving a lot of sick in town.[5] Camped for the night.
Aug	29"	Began the return march. My shoes went to pieces, and I had a hard day. We made 28 miles during the day.[6]

---

[4] Monroe is in Ouachita Parish, Louisiana.

[5] Confederate Brigadier General Paul Octave Hébert (1818-1880) had retreated across the Ouachita River (Winters, *The Civil War in Louisiana*, 302; Warner, *Generals in Gray*, 131-132).

[6] That night they camped at Oak Ridge in Morehouse Parish (*Downing's Civil War Diary*, 139).

Aug	30"	Marched 7 miles and camped on Boe[u]f River. Along with about a hundred others I had a hard chill, from drinking bad water.
Aug	31	Left Beouf river at an early hour. My feet were so sore I had to ride about 2 miles, at 3 P.M. camped at Bayou Mason after 17 miles.[7]
Sept	1"	Lying over during the day at Bayou Mason. Had another chill, with high fever and headache. Watermellons and green corn were issued to us. We have had plenty to eat. Orders to start at midnight.
Sept	2^d	Marched at midnight last night and kept it up until 9 A.M. All hands were glad to see the old Mississippi.
Sept	3^d	We went on board the Sam Gatz and steamed away for Vicksburg. Arrived at 4 P.M. We had a good supper, cleaned up some, and felt like new men. My malarial attack is much better. Found letters from Amelia and Mother.

---

[7] Bayou Macon is a tributary of the Tensas River.

Chapter X
"We are very comfortably situated just now"
Vicksburg
September to December 1863

For the most part the regiment performed garrison duty around Vicksburg for the remainder of the year. On 20 September the Third Division, of which the Eleventh and the Iowa Brigade were a part, became the First Division of the XVII Army Corps.[1] During this period Will suffered periodically from "fever and ague" or malaria.

Sept	4	Spent the time resting up from the hard trip, and putting things in order again. Answered my letters.
Sept	5"	Am on camp guard today. It seems a little dry after being on the move. I [am] reading an Encyclopedia I found at "Oakhill" on the Monroe march.[2]
Sept	6"	Have been busy all day fixing up a water tank. After having so much nice fresh vegetables lately, our camp rations seem a bit dry.
Sept	7"	Letters today from Robert and Amelia. Nothing happened worth recording.
Sept	8"	The Regiment at this time is the smallest it has ever been, only 25 in the company fit for duty. Nearly all troops gone from Vicksburg but our Division.

---

[1] *Downing's Civil War Diary*, 143.

[2] "Oakhill" was probably Oak Ridge, Louisiana. Fultz referred to the place as Oakland, "oak" apparently being the common denominator.

*Will's brother, Robert D. Wade
(Courtesy of Nina Anderson)*

Sept 10"   Have orders to move inside the lines tomorrow.

Sept 11"   Made an early start and went through the city, toward the South about 2 or 3 miles out on the Warrenton road. [N]ear some old rebel works we made our camp.

Sept 12"   Sharp and I found an old reb powder magazine ceiled with pine lumber. We stood in powder four inches deep and knocked it off, carried it to camp and built tables, bunks, shelves &c.

Sept 13"   Our company went on picket today[.] It took Major Pamootz[3] about two hours to tell us where to go. While on the line we heard an explosion and saw a great cloud of dust going up. A negro

---

[3] George Pomutz (1818-1882) was a major and later lieutenant colonel of the Fifteenth Iowa Infantry. A native of Hungary, he was later U.S. consul in St. Petersburg, Russia (John H. Eicher, and David J. Eicher, *Civil War High Commands* [Stanford, Calif.: Stanford University Press, 2001], 433; 1860 U.S. census, Decatur County, Iowa, pop. sch., New Buda, p. 87, dwel. 636, fam. 601, George Pomutz; NARA micro. publ. M653, roll 318).

sergeant had walked into the powder magazine where Sharp and I found our lumber[. H]e thought he would take a quiet little smoke! They picked a good deal of him up[.][4] Letters from Amelia and Grandfather.

Major George Pomutz (State Historical Society of Iowa)

Sept 14"   After fighting mosquitoes all night I came off picket, did not get an hours sleep all night.

Sept 15"   Our three years will be out one year and one month from today. The time is slipping away very rapidly.

Sept 16"   Companies A and B returned from Lake Providence where they went after an Engine.[5]

---

[4] This incident was also recorded the following month by a lieutenant in the Fifteenth Iowa (Edward Rynearson Michaels, ed., *The Civil War Letters of Sylvester Rynearson, 1861-1865* [E. R. Michaels, 1981], 123).

[5] Downing indicated that this was a foraging expedition (*Downing's Civil War Diary*, 142).

Sept	17"	My Birthday anniversary. I am keeping it by standing guard. We are very comfortably situated just now, but a soldier is never sure about anything.
Sept	18"	The weather has turned suddenly cool, and overcoats are being hunted up, and tents made more snug.
Sept	19"	Our Q.M. doled out some Sanitary stuff today, just to ease his conscience a little[,] the 25" Iowa has had plenty of it.
Sept	20"	This morning our company had to go on duty to double the pickets, Gen. Sherman having sent orders to look out for an attack on the morning of the 21".
Sept	21"	The day was a hot uncomfortable one and dragged away at last, but no rebs came, and at evening we were relieved of duty.
Sept	22^d	Hummell went to the city, and brought some real butter back. We felt like "nabobs[.]"
Sept	23	Had a letter from Mother, all well there.
Sept	24"	Went on guard this morning, did not feel very well. In the evening had a chill and had to ask to be relieved.
Sept	25"	Had fever nearly all last night, later began sweating. Bathed a good deal and felt some better.
Sept	26"	Reported sick, and was marked off duty.
Sept	27"	Went on picket near an old rebel powder magazine. Had a lot of fun filling ratholes with the

		powder and seeing the rats scamper when we touched them off.
Sept	28	Came off picket rather late, did not feel very well, have Malaria.
Sept	29"	Went to the city for a short time. On my return stopped at the M.M.B. Hospt and saw Kingsbury. He was laid up sick.[6]
Sept	30	On picket again. Rained last night and drizzled most of today. We built us a shed and kept dry and comfortable.
Oct	1"	The Grand Review came off today, and we had to wait till nearly 10 AM.[7]
Oct	2^d	On picket again, This makes three nights with very little sleep for me.
Oct	3^d	Got off picket early. We drew clothing. I am hoping to see the greenback wagon soon.
Oct	4"	Review today by Gen McPherson. It was a good show, but I did not feel at all well and was very tired when it was over. Battle of Corinth one year ago today.

---

[6] Madison M. Kingsbury. See Appendix B. The Mississippi Marine Brigade hospital was located on the ship *Woodford* (Hearn, *Ellet's Brigade*, 145, 183; Warren D. Crandall and Isaac D. Newell, *History of the Ram Fleet and the Mississippi Marine Brigade in the War for the Union* [St. Louis: Buschart, 1907], 379).

[7] Downing described this as brigade inspection by General McArthur beginning at seven in the morning. Hence Will's complaint about waiting till ten (*Downing's Civil War Diary*, 145).

Oct	5	On picket near the river today. I enjoyed it very much.
Oct	6"	Came off picket. In the afternoon marched to town and were reviewed by Gen Grant. Just at night we were called into line and the regiment had to lie on arms all night. It rained and stormed all night. It was a tough old time.
Oct	7	Relieved by the 13' at 1 P.M. I spent the afternoon in the river bottom hunting wild grapes, found plenty and had a good time.
Oct	8"	Regiment on picket duty. I was on outpost duty. Had a more pleasant time than before.
Oct	9"	The 13' came out promptly and relieved us. We carried a lot of lumber, working hard all day, we rearranged our bunks, one above another like a steamer.
Oct	10"	On picket again. In the evening had orders to march at 6 A.M.
Oct	11"	Did not start until 7 A.M. and then went about 7 miles out of our road. Made the river before dark, but all were tired.[8]
Oct	12"	It has rained today, we had to work building a shelter, before it was done I was drenched to the skin.
Oct	13	All Iowa soldiers voted today, for state officers.[9] Afterward I visited the 4" Iowa Cav. and took dinner with Uncle Jonathan.

---

[8] The Eleventh marched to Black River Bridge.

Oct	14	Went graping in the forenoon, returning to camp found marching orders. At 2 P.M. went moved to the camp of the 5 Minn. And occupied their tents, ours had good bunks.[10]
Oct	15	It is two years today since we were mustered into service at Davenport Iowa. This is a beautiful day. It has been a long time since I received letters.
Oct	16"	I am guarding the commissary today. Uncle Jonathan visited me. Beautiful day.
Oct	17"	Came off guard feeling very tired. Gen. Chambers closed the bakeries to keep soldiers from eating soft bread.[11]
Oct	18	Had company inspection. Later I visited the 4" Iowa Cav. had a good dinner, and afterward a pleasant ride.
Oct	19"	The troops who were out on a march returned, and we had to give up their tents and camp in the woods where we were before.[12]

---

[9] Republican William Stone received 236 votes, compared with the Democrat General Tuttle, who received only 11. Stone had been colonel of the Twenty-second Iowa (Fultz MS, 64; *Downing's Civil War Diary*, 147).

[10] The Fifth Minnesota Infantry had left on an expedition to Canton, Mississippi (Fultz MS, 64; *Downing's Civil War Diary*, 147).

[11] Alexander Chambers, colonel of the Sixteenth Iowa, was at this time commander of the Iowa Brigade ("General Alexander Chambers").

[12] In other words, the Fifth Minnesota wanted their camp back (see Fultz MS, 64).

Oct	20"	Logans division marched in today on their road to Vicksburg. They did not accomplish anything while out.[13]
Oct	21"	Marched at 6 A.M. for Vicksburg. Arrived there at 2 P.M. pretty tired and hungry. Found letter from Wade.
Oct	22^d	Spent the day washing and mending my "wardrobe[.]" Many of the boys have received clothes (socks and underwear[)] from home. They are better than we get here.
Oct	23^d	It began to rain in the night and has kept it up slowly all day. Not good weather for soldiering. It is reported that the 2^d Brigade is here.[14]
Oct	24	On picket near the river, weather sharp and frosty. Signed payrolls, and will probably be paid off soon.
Oct	25"	Came off picket and found a letter from Amelia. In the evening we attended the Presbyterian Church. Enjoyed the services very much.[15]

---

[13] General John Alexander Logan (1826-1886) was in command of the Third Division of the XVII Corps. This division was engaged in skirmishes near Brownsville, Hinds County, Mississippi 15-17 October 1863 (Warner, *Generals in Blue*, 281-283; *OR* 30 [2], 808-809).

[14] The Second Brigade, under General Ransom, included the Eleventh Illinois, Wade Matthews' regiment.

[15] The pastor of the Presbyterian Church in Vicksburg at the time was Edwin H. Rutherford (1831-1908). A native of Tennessee, he was in Vicksburg from 1857 to 1866. Will seemed to like his preaching, as he attended services several times that fall (see Frank E. Everett, Jr., *A History of the First Presbyterian Church of Vicksburg in the Nineteenth Century* [Vicksburg: 1980], iii, 51, 73, 87-88; Rev. Edwin H. Rutherford obituary, *The* [Paris, Kentucky] *Bourbon News*, 31 July 1908, p. 1, c. 1).

Dr. William Matthews, Wade Matthews' father (Courtesy of Jananne Slaughter)

Oct 26" Saw Wade today, he was well. Read a letter from his father.[16] I hope his company will be reinstated soon. Wade is P.M. of 11"[.][17]

Oct 27" We received our pay today for two months. I sent $10. to Mother.

Oct 28 I put in the day changing the pockets in my trousers.

---

[16] Wade's father was Dr. William Matthews of Effingham, Mason County, Illinois (William Henry Perrin, *History of Effingham County, Illinois* [Chicago: Baskin, 1883], 164).

[17] According to his service record, Wade Matthews was placed under arrest and in confinement 1 March 1863 and was restored to duty in March 1864, at which time he was made regimental postmaster. It could be that Will hoped that Wade would be reinstated. (Compiled service record, D. Wade Matthews, Pvt., Co. G, 11 Illinois Inf.; Carded Records, Volunteer Organizations, Civil War; Records of the Adjutant General's Office, 1780s-1917, Record Group 94, National Archives, Washington, D.C.).

Oct	29"	Went to town with detail to work on the new line of intrenchments. I ate my dinner at a restaurant. In the evening went to camp in a rain.
Oct	30"	It began to rain very heavily this morning by 10 A.M. it was running through the tents and rising rapidly. We had to get out the best we could, carrying things on our backs and wading waist deep. Some very laughable things happened.
Oct	31"	Mustered for pay, for Sept. and Oct. In the evening had orders to move camp.
Nov	1"	We packed up our things and moved about three quarters of a mile. I had to move all of our stuff alone.
Nov	2^d	On camp guard. Lonesome old business. Frank Daily returned bringing a lot of nice things for the New London boys.[18]
Nov	3^d	Came off guard, and spent the day grading the company streets, am feeling very well.
Nov	4"	Went on a visit to Wade, found him well, and had a pleasant time. Met Capt. Easton of the 8" La A.D.[19]

---

[18] Francis M. Daily. See Appendix B.

[19] Orlando W. Easton (1837-1913) was a New York native from Columbus City in Louisa County. He was originally a color sergeant in Co. C, Eleventh Iowa. He was appointed captain of Co. H, Eighth Louisiana Infantry African Descent in May 1863. That regiment became the Forty-seventh U.S. Colored Infantry, stationed in the Vicksburg area. He resigned in March 1864 (*Roster and Record*, 316; Compiled service record, Orlando W. Easton, Capt., Co. H, 47 U.S.C.T. Inf.; Carded Records, Volunteer Organizations, Civil War; Records of the Adjutant General's Office, 1780s-1917, Record Group 94, National Archives, Washington, D.C.; California death index 1905-1929, microfilm no. 1,686,044, Family History Library, Salt Lake City, Utah).

Nov	5"	It has rained all day. A regular November day. Our tent leaked some.
Nov	7"	Went on the intrenchment detail again, worked hard all day. At noon I went to a restaurant, and satisfied the inner man.
Nov	8"	Attended the Catholic church at 11 A.M. Some of the performances were so queer, that some of the boys lost their gravity[.] At evening attended Presbyterian church.
Nov	9"	I helped haul a load of wood, and did some sewing on my clothes. Drew an overcoat $9.57[.]
Nov	10"	Attended the Literary Society down town and heard some able speeches.[20]
Nov	12	Built a fireplace to warm our tent, it draws well and heats our tent thoroughly.
Nov	13'	Carried lumber from an old fort about 3/4 of a mile from camp. Arch went back to town. Had a letter from Amelia, and answered it at once.
Nov	14"	Am on picket. A very pleasant day. Lieut Foster was with us.
Nov	15"	Came off picket this morning. Went to church in the evening. Heard a good sermon.

---

[20] The soldiers stationed around Vicksburg for the winter organized the Vicksburg Union Literary Association, which met weekly and included debates, readings and the presentation of essays by the members. See Hampton Smith, *Brother of Mine: the Civil War Letters of Thomas and William Christies* (Minnesota Historical Society, 2011), 182.

Nov	16"	We had a Grammar School at night. It was quite instructive. Letter from Uncle Solon.
Nov	17"	Helped to haul two loads of wood. It made me good and tired. Signed pay rolls for Sept and Oct. Answered Solons letter.
Nov	19"	Helped haul brick for a company furnace to cook on.
Nov	20"	Wrote to Mother sending $10. and to Robert sending 5. Were paid $26.
Nov	21"	Visited the city, and went sightseeing for several hours.
Nov	22^d	On picket near the river. A cool breezy day.
Nov	23^d	Came off picket, not feeling very well. Had taken cold, and felt stiff and sore.
Nov	24"	A stormy old time. Raining and blowing great guns. Glad to be in camp poor as that is.
Nov	26"	Went into town and took a shave and shampoo.[21] Afterward went to church heard a good Thanksgiving sermon.
Nov	27	Sharp and I went to town. I bought a book so as to have something to read. The city is getting in better shape. All kinds of stores and shops are being opened up.

---

[21] At this time the term "shampoo" meant a massage as much as washing the hair and was often associated with a haircut. See "Shampoo," in *The Compact Edition of the Oxford English Dictionary* (Oxford University Press, 1971), 2:2768.

Nov	28"	While we were fixing up today our tent caught fire, but we soon had it out. Wade visited me. The weather is cold.
Nov	29"	Wade came over, and we attended church together. Heard a good sermon.
Nov	30	On guard today. Had a letter from Grandfather.
Dec	1"	Came off guard with a severe cold. Had to go to bed. My lungs quite sore and I perspired freely[.]
Dec	4"	Went to town to get some potatoes, but failed to find any, we pay $4.$^{00/100}$ per barrel. In the evening Siberts and Lockwood came back from Iowa, Bringing many things for the company.[22] I got a pair of boots, socks and a shirt. I also had a letter from Robert.
Dec	6"	On camp guard. Nothing worthy of note today.
Dec	7	Nicodemus brought out some fine potatoes from town let me have a barrel for $1.60[.][23] They are from the North and very fine.
Dec	8	Worked a good part of the day repairing our tent. Drew some clothes. Trousers Blouse, knapsack and haversack $6.69[.]
Dec	10"	Had charge of a squad of Provo[st] guards[.][24] Found a lot of soldiers fighting, and my men bayonetted a man.

---

[22] Edward Siberts and Edwin J. Lockwood. See Appendix B.

[23] William H. Nicodemus. See Appendix B.

[24] The Eleventh provided a captain, a lieutenant, two sergeants, eight corporals (including Will) and forty privates for the patrol for Vicksburg that day (*Downing's Civil War Diary*, 157).

Dec	11	Col. Abercrombie sent for me, and inquired very thoroughly into the affair last night. He did not blame me, but the mans friends were hostile[.]
Dec	12	Went into town and had a tailor alter my new blouse and pantaloons cost me $1.50. Had pockets changed.
Dec	13"	Force and I attended church in the evening. Good sermon.
Dec	15"	On Brigade guard. Weather bright and pleasant for this time of year.
Dec	16"	It began to rain in the night, and all our things got a wetting.
Dec	17"	Made a visit to Wade and had a very pleasant day with him and with some others of his company.
Dec	[1]8"	The orders about cooking came out on Dress parade. I was out part of the day looking for brick.
Dec	20	Attended church twice at the Presbyterian church. It was very enjoyable.
Dec	22^d	On Provo[st] guard duty today. There were a good many drunk men, but we had no trouble to keep things quiet. There was a fine meeting of the Literary Society. Had a letter from Mother.
Dec	24"	Wade made me a visit, and remained till morning. Just at night got orders to march with two days rations. Answered Mothers letter.

Dec	25	Started at 11 P.M. last night and arrived at Redbone at 3 A.M.[25] We laid armed all day. All hands were in a bad frame of mind, as it seemed to be a useless trip.
Dec	26	Started on the return trip at 2 P.M. and reached camp at 6 P.M. tired hungry and "<u>cross</u>"[.] Yesterday was our <u>third</u> and <u>last</u> Christmas in the Army.[26]
Dec	27	Worked on my rifle nearly all day.
Dec	29	Am on Headquarter guard with Sergt McNeely. The day a pleasant one[.] Received a letter from A.E.C. in answer to mine of July 6", a good friendly letter[.]
Dec	30	Began raining about relief time and kept it up all day. Could not attend the Literary Society Meeting. Had letters from Amelia and Grandfather.
Dec	31	It is a stormy ending of the year. A cold rain is falling, and the wind is blowing a gale.

---

[25] Redbone is in Warren County, about 12 miles south of Vicksburg. At the time it consisted of about three or four houses and a church. The Fifteenth and Eleventh Iowa were both detailed under the Fifteenth's Colonel Belknap to reinforce the Second Wisconsin Cavalry and Sixteenth Wisconsin Infantry from a possible Confederate attack. As it was a false alarm, the soldiers felt it was a diversion so that the officers who remained at Vicksburg could celebrate the holidays (Fultz MS, 67; Michaels, *Sylvester Rynearson Letters*, 134-135; *Downing's Civil War Diary*, 159).

[26] Most of the Eleventh chose to re-enlist as veteran volunteers during December, earning a bounty and a thirty day furlough. Indeed, this was encouraged in many regiments, as Will's uncle Jonathan re-enlisted in the Fourth Iowa Cavalry on 15 December. Will's emphasis on this being his last Christmas in the army is indicative of his desire not to re-enlist.

Chapter XI
Filling the Gap:
The Meridian Expedition and the Iowa Battalion
January to May 1864

After his 31 December 1863 entry, Will's journal is blank for the next six months, resuming 29 June 1864. When it picks up again, it appears that Will had been making entries all along, indicating that he probably lost that portion of his diaries. However, he left eight blank pages in the copied journal, probably intending to fill in later. According to his military records, Will was present with his regiment during the entire period his journal is silent. It is therefore possible to reconstruct his whereabouts and activity from other sources, those for the Iowa Brigade in general and the Eleventh Regiment in particular.

Significantly, Will was reduced in ranks, losing his corporal's stripes, as of 1 January 1864, the day the gap in the journal begins. Some editing on Will's part is possible. His demotion was probably in response to the incident in December when one of the provost guards in his detail bayoneted a soldier.

The month of January 1864 was a continuation of the previous few months. Remaining part of the garrison at Vicksburg, the regiment spent its time between picket duty, provost guard in the city, and lying around in camp. The re-enlistment of veteran volunteers continued in the early days of the month. Initially, soldiers re-enlisting for another three years would receive a large bounty, as well as a thirty-day furlough. The War Department, however, rescinded that order as of midnight, 5 January 1864. As a result, most of the re-enlistments took place before the expiration of the bounty. Enough soldiers re-enlisted that the Eleventh became a veteran regiment, being mustered in as such on 25 January.[1] Will was among those that chose not to re-enlist, so that, if he lived, his term of service would expire in October 1864.

The furloughs granted the veteran volunteers were put on hold, however, as General Sherman had more immediate plans.

---

[1] *Downing's Civil War Diary*, 161-163.

Before he lost too many soldiers to furloughs, and before the spring campaign season began, Sherman wished to strike at the rail center and supply base at Meridian, Mississippi. Located one hundred thirty-five miles from Vicksburg, near the Alabama border, Meridian contained large stores of supplies as well as an armory and hospital. Destroying those stores as well as the railroad there could disrupt Confederate movements and effectually take Mississippi out of the war.[2]

Sherman planned to strike against Meridian quickly, and therefore he proceeded without the usual supply lines. His force would rely solely on what they could carry and what they could forage from the countryside. The significance of this march is that it was in a sense a practice for Sherman's more famous, or infamous, March to the Sea. It also demonstrated Sherman's development of the policy of "hard war."[3]

Taking three divisions from the XVI and XVII Army Corps each, in addition to four regiments of cavalry, Sherman's force consisted of over twenty-six hundred soldiers. Will and the Eleventh Iowa, as part of the Iowa Brigade under the command of Brigadier General Alexander Chambers, were included in that number. Also along on the expedition were two of Will's uncles, Jonathan Jessup of the Fourth Iowa Cavalry and Samuel Merrill Jessup of the Thirty-third Missouri Infantry.[4]

The cavalry brigade, under the command of Edward F. Winslow, left Vicksburg on 3 February 1864. The Iowa Brigade, leaving the next day, was initially in the rear of the expedition, but

---

[2] Buck T. Foster, *Sherman's Mississippi Campaign* (Tuscaloosa: University of Alabama Press, 2006), 14-31. See also William Forse Scott, *The Story of a Cavalry Regiment: The Career of the Fourth Iowa Veteran Volunteers: From Kansas to Georgia, 1861-1865* (New York: Putnam's, 1893), 185.

[3] Foster, *Sherman's Mississippi Campaign*, 21, 28, 168. Steven E. Woodworth, *Nothing But Victory: the Army of the Tennessee, 1861-1865* (New York: Vintage Books, 2005), 480-481.

[4] Composition of the Meridian Expedition, *OR* 32 (1), 170-172; Compiled military service record, Jonathan Jessup, Sgt., Co. D, 4 Ia. Cav., Civil War, RG 94, NA-Washington; Compiled military service record, Samuel M. Jessup, Corp., Co. F, 33 Mo. Inf., Civil War, RG 94, NA-Washington.

was generally in second position for most of the campaign. There was skirmishing for the first week as the expedition moved towards Jackson and Meridian, mostly involving the cavalry, but with some infantry support. On 7 February the Eleventh was in the advance and after reaching Brandon, Companies C and D began destroying the railroad. On 9 February at Morton the Eleventh tore up about a mile and a half of track, burning ties and twisting rails. This work continued as the army proceeded to Meridian, which it reached 15 February. Destruction continued in earnest around Meridian. The infantry was busy tearing up railroads, as well as destroying rolling stock, warehouses and other buildings, including some residences.[5] In order to destroy both the Mobile & Ohio and the Jackson & Selma railroads, General Stephen A. Hurlbut's XVI Corps concentrated north and east of town while General James B. McPherson's XVII Corps worked to the south and west.[6] When they were done General Sherman reported that "Meridian, with its depots, store-houses, arsenal, hospitals, offices, hotels, and cantonments no longer exists."[7] The expedition began the return march on 20 February and reached Vicksburg on 4 March 1864. The Iowa Brigade marched a total of 365 miles, destroyed 6 3/4 miles of track, one bridge, nineteen locomotives, eighteen railroad cars, and 165 feet of trestle-work at the cost of two men killed, two wounded and fourteen missing.[8]

After the return to Vicksburg the re-enlisted veterans began making preparations for their thirty-day furloughs and heading back to Iowa. The Thirteenth Iowa left on 7 March. The Fifteenth and Eleventh Iowa veterans boarded the steamer "Continental" on 13 March.[9]

---

[5] Fultz MS, 68-69; *Downing's Civil War Diary*, 168.

[6] Woodworth, *Nothing But Victory*, 484.

[7] Report of Major General W. T. Sherman, *OR* 32 (1), 176.

[8] Report of Major General James B. McPherson, *OR* 32 (1), 212.

[9] *Downing's Civil War Diary*, 173-174; Michaels, *Civil War Letters of Sylvester Rynearson*, 145.

The non-veterans of the Iowa Brigade were gathered into the "Iowa Battalion" commanded by Major George Pomutz of the Fifteenth Iowa. It left Vicksburg on 30 March and traveled to Cairo, Illinois, arrived 3 April. The Battalion remained in garrison there and at Mound City, Illinois, spending most of their time drilling. At Cairo it joined a division composed of returning veterans under the command of General Walter Q. Gresham. The Battalion left Cairo for Clifton, Tennessee on 28 April 1864, traveling up the Tennessee River aboard the steamboat "Collesus." On 5 May it proceeded overland to Huntsville, Alabama, arriving on 20 May. Gresham's force took along 3,000 head of cattle for Sherman's army, 900 of which were under the care of the Iowa Battalion.

At Huntsville the Iowa Battalion joined the balance of the XVII Corps, now under the command of General Frank P. Blair, as General McPherson had been promoted to command of the Army of the Tennessee. The Iowa Brigade was reunited between 22 and 24 May and became the Third Brigade, Colonel Hall of the Eleventh commanding, in General Marcellus Crocker's Fourth Division. Lieutenant Colonel Abercrombie rose then to the command of the Eleventh Iowa.[10]

---

[10] S. H. M. Byers, *Iowa in War Times* (Des Moines: W. D. Condit & Co., 1888), 505; Matilda Gresham, *Life of Walter Quintin Gresham, 1832-1895* (Chicago: Rand McNally, 1919), 294-296; Jennings, *My Story*, 26-28; *Downing's Civil War Diary*, 190; Fultz MS, 78.

Chapter XII
"A Storm of Shot and Shell"
The Atlanta Campaign
May to September 1864

The Eleventh left Huntsville on 25 May. Marching through Decatur and Somerville, Alabama, they had reached Rome, Georgia by 5 June. The next day they continued the march through Kingston and Cartersville and arrived in camp at Acworth on 8 June. It was on that day that the XVII Corps joined Sherman's army.

Sherman had assembled three armies for the campaign against Atlanta, the Army of the Cumberland under General George Thomas, the Army of the Ohio under General John Pope, and the Army of the Tennessee under General James B. McPherson. The campaign had begun 7 May, as each of the three armies moved toward Johnston at Dalton, Georgia. Sherman's forces advanced as Johnston retreated south, with significant engagements at Resaca and New Hope Church.[1] *The Army of the Tennessee, now including the XVII Corps, formed the left flank of Sherman's forces as he resumed their advance on 10 June.*[2] *From Acworth, the Eleventh moved on Big Shanty, eight miles distant, skirmishing with the enemy the last three miles. The Eleventh dug in and were about four miles from Kennesaw Mountain. The regiment was in full view of the Confederate flag as it "floated to the breeze" from the mountaintop.*[3] *Skirmishing continued for the next five or six days, as did the rain.*[4] *The Eleventh slowly advanced toward the enemy, one mile on 11 June, one half mile on*

---

[1] For an account of the campaign before the Eleventh arrived, see Jacob D. Cox, *Atlanta* (NewYork: Charle Scribner's Sons, 1882), 33-88.

[2] Albert Castel, *Decision in the West: the Atlanta Campaign of 1864* (Lawrence: University of Kansas Press, 1992), 269.

[3] Fultz MS, 81.

[4] *Downing's Civil War Diary*, 195-198; Mifflin Jennings, 10-16 June 1864.

12 June, digging rifle pits and building breastworks as they went.[5] The skirmish line was again advanced on 23 June, and Companies E, F and G spent twenty-four hours as skirmishers until relieved by the Fifteenth Iowa on the evening of 25 June.[6] On 27 June the Union army advanced on all fronts. The XVII Corps, with the Army of the Tennessee, were repulsed. The only companies of the Eleventh engaged that day were A and H. They sustained two killed and three wounded in the assault.[7] The following day Companies C, D, E, F and G were on picket duty.[8]

Thus were the affairs of the Eleventh Iowa when Will's record resumes.

1864

June	29"	Our company went on picket at dark, the line was quiet.
June	30"	During the night there was heavy artillery firing on the right. At times as rapid as rifle fire.
July	1"	Mustered for pay today, for May and June. This makes six months pay due us.
July	2^d	Orders to march at a moments notice[.] After dark we moved to the right.
July	3^d	Marched all of last night. Halted just after daylight and ate our breakfast. Started soon after for the extreme right, reached there at 2 P.M. rested until 4 P.M. when we moved to the front.

---

[5] Fultz MS, 81-82.

[6] *Downing's Civil War Diary*, 200-201.

[7] Fultz MS, 85-86.

[8] Mifflin Jennings, 28 June 1864.

		Drove the enemy back until dusk, then fell back 3/4 of a mile and camped.
July	4	The 15" and 16" pushed the enemy until noon when the 11" and 13 took the front. Our company were sent out as skirmishers.[9] We drove them on the run over hills and through brush into their works and within 75 yards of the guns, which we silenced. At dusk we fell back with a loss of 2 killed, and 8 wounded.
July	5"	Our Brigade charged the fort, and drove them out, we reformed our lines and advanced about 12 o'c[lock]. we came in sight of their works we halted until 4 P.M. then under cover of a rapid artillery fire advanced to within half mile were met with so severe an artillery fire of Brooks guns that we halted and laid down.[10] Our 10" Ohio ran up a section by hand, but could not hold their position. Gen Gresham and Col. Hall were drunk and quarreled, the field officers conferred and refused to charge the works.[11] Started a line of works[.]

---

[9] Three companies each from the Eleventh and Thirteenth Iowa under Major Charles Foster of the Eleventh were sent out as skirmishers, alternating shifts with skirmishers from the Fifteenth and Sixteenth (Fultz MS, 89).

[10] Will may have had trouble reading his original entry, mistaking "Brooks" for "Shoups." General Francis A. Shoup (1834-1896) was Johnston's chief of artillery and the one responsible for constructing the Confederate fortifications at Nickajack Creek (Gen. F. A. Shoup, "Dalton Campaign -- Works at Chattahoochee River -- Interesting History," *Confederate Veteran*, v. 3, no. 9 [September 1895], 262-265; see also Warner, *Generals in Gray*, 275-276).

[11] Brigadier General Walter Quintin Gresham (1832-1895) was in command of the Fourth Division of the XVII Corps until 20 July when he was wounded in the knee. He later held cabinet posts under Presidents Arthur and Cleveland (Warner, *Generals in Blue*, 188-189; Fultz MS, 88).

July	6"	Worked all night, and by morning had a good line built.
July	7"	G. reported for picket. While at Brig. Hdqrs. the rebs opened a storm of shot and shell, we laid flat on the ground and let them go it. Co. F lost 1 killed.[12]
July	8"	Put in the day firing at the pits, would see a man occasionally for a minute.
July	9"	Rather a quiet day. I took a bath in stream[.]
July	10	This morning the rebs line of heavy works was deserted, about 8 A.M. the 11" and 13 marched over and took possession. It was Cleburns men.[13] Lieut Foster returned looking very well.
July	11"	Rather quiet today.
July	12"	Ordered to police camp, and camp for a few days. Are finding some fine blackberries.
July	13	Took a dip in the branch, coming out got orders to move, marched about a mile and camped[.]
July	14	Had a letter from Mother, dated June 27.
July	16	Marched at 5 P.M. toward Marietta. Reached there at midnight.

---

[12] Probably Corporal Thomas M. Souter (or Suitor, 1830-1864), a Scottish native from Washington, Iowa, who was wounded 7 July and died the following day (*Roster and Record*, 2:383).

[13] Major General Patrick Ronayne Cleburne (1828-1864) commanded a division in the Confederate Army of Tennessee. A native of Ireland, he was killed four months later at the Battle of Franklin (Warner, *Generals in Gray*, 53-54).

July	17"	Marched through Marietta and crossed the Chattahoochee at Russ's Mills.[14] Camped 4 miles beyond.
July	18"	Marched 10 miles and camped for the night[.]
July	19"	Marched to within 3 miles of Decatur and camped.
July	20	Marched through Decatur. The railroad was being destroyed. About a mile beyond formed line and drove the rebels into their works. Co. "E" lost one man killed.[15]
July	21	Our corps charged the works and secured a better position. 11" was in second line [.][16] Brig lost about 200 killed & wounded. Hudson was killed. We built a line of works. Afterward moved to left and built another line.
July	22^d	Rebels evacuated their lines held yesterday. I went with a strong detail from the 11" to build a new line to the left and front. About 12.30 heard firing in the rear, and were told to join the regiment. Several made it. Geo McNeely was captured. The Brigade was first on one side and then the other. After a stubborn fight lasting till dark were driven back to Bald knob, where a new line was formed

---

[14] Probably Roswell Mill which was a center of cotton and woolen mills located on the Chattahoochee River at the modern city of Roswell (Fultz MS, 95).

[15] David Hobaugh (1840-1864), Comapny E, was an Indiana native from Clinton County who had been captured at Corinth 4 October 1862 and re-enlisted as a Veteran Volunteer (*Roster and Record*, 332; *Downing's Civil War Diary*, 206n).

[16] Fultz indicates that the Iowa Brigade charged alone and unsupported, the Thirteenth and Fifteenth regiments forming the front line and the Eleventh and Sixteenth the rear (Fultz MS, 96).

at right angles to the one occupied in the morning, here we held our ground until night when the fight was over. Company loss, 3 killed, 5 wounded 13 captured.[17]

July 23 Enemy withdrew during night leaving dead and some wounded. Capt. Bohn Co. "B" C.S.A. who headed the assault at the Knob, laid within 40 feet of our works.[18]

July 24 Strengthened our works. Building traverses. Had letter from Mother.

July 25 Visited 13", found Frank Farley missing, other friends all right.[19]

July 26 Laid in camp till night, ordered to march[.] But did not move till midnight.

July 27 Marched all night, halted in field near 4" corps for breakfast.[20] Moved into position.

---

[17] See report of Lt. Col. Abercrombie, *OR* I:38, pt. 3, 599-600.

[18] Captain William F. Bourne of Company B, Third Confederate Infantry was killed on the assault on Bald Knob. A native of Ohio, he was raised in Memphis, Tennessee (Compiled service record, Wm. F. Bourne, Capt., Co. B, 3 Confederate Inf.; Carded Records, Volunteer Organizations, Civil War; Records of the Adjutant General's Office, 1780s-1917, Record Group 94, National Archives, Washington, D.C.; 1860 U.S. census, Shelby Co., Tennessee, pop. sch., Memphis, p. 158 [stamped], dwel. 994, fam. 1045, Jas T Bourne; NARA micro. publ. M653, roll 1273).

[19] Francis H. Farley (1841-1922), Co. I, Thirteenth Iowa Infantry, from Washington, Iowa, was captured 22 July 1864 (*Roster and Record*, 612; Francis H. Farley, *Organization Index to Pension Files of Veterans who served between 1861 and 1900*).

[20] At Peachtree Creek (Fultz MS, 98).

July	28	Advanced with some skirmishing to our line and threw up works, Just then enemy charged Logans corps (15")[.] We expected one, and shells and balls came over us. After a hard fight they were repulsed with heavy loss said to be 3000. Logans corps lost about 150. They shelled us every 15 minutes all night.[21]
July	29"	Gov. Stone visited all the Iowa troops but our regiment. We felt slighted.[22]
July	30	Moved to the right into works already built the smell from shallow buried dead was so great we could not eat. Holloway and I put on dirt.[23]
July	31	Company on picket a rainy day.
Aug	1"	Came off picket feeling sick. I think the foul air from dead men and animals caused it.
Aug	2ᵈ	Moved over to our new works, in the evening drew clothing. I drew gum & canteen.
Aug	4"	Whole picket line was advanced, some fighting[.]

---

[21] This engagement was the Battle of Ezra Church (see James L. McDonough and James Pickett Jones, *War so terrible: Sherman and Atlanta* [New York: Norton, 1987], 257-260; Castel, *Decision in the West*, 426-430).

[22] Governor William M. Stone (1827-1893) was a New York born attorney in Knoxville, Marion County, Iowa before the war. He enlisted in 1861, becoming a major in the Third Iowa Infantry. Gov. Kirkwood later appointed him colonel of the Twenty-second Iowa Infantry. He was elected governor while still in the army, serving 1864-1868 (*Portrait and Biographical Record of Henry County, Iowa*, 131-132; Gue, *History of Iowa*, 4:253).

[23] Harrison Holloway. See Appendix B.

Aug	5"	About 9 P.M. Rebs opened up with artillery, we laid ready for them, but they did not come on[.] Company on picket, no firing near us.
Aug	6	Rebels were noisy, singing and yelling the greater part of the night.
Aug	7"	During afternoon rebs artillery was active. About 10 P.M. were called up by fighting on the right. It soon quieted down again, constant vigilance and loss of sleep are telling on us.
Aug	9"	At 4 four companies of 11" including "G," went to build a new line for the Brigade near rebel batteries.[24] Went into camp.
Aug	10"	Artillery firing all day.
Aug	11"	Began a new line of works during the day[.] Man belonging to pioneer corps killed. 1 of Co. "I" mortally 1 of Co. "H" badly wounded by sharpshooters.[25]
Aug	14"	Wrote 8 page account of the July 22^d battle to the Mt Pleasant Journal.[26]

---

[24] The four companies were F, G, H, and I. They finished the breastworks begun the day before by companies K, A, B, C and D (Fultz MS, 103).

[25] Henry Hazelton (1843-1864), Company I, was wounded severely in the abdomen on 12 August and died the following day. He was a native of Pennsylvania from Muscatine County.
  Jasper W. Shoemaker (1840-) of Louisa County, Company H, was wounded 12 August (*Roster and Record*, 336, 386; Baker, *Report*, 1:641, 643).

[26] Unfortunately, as of November 2011, there are no known extant copies of the Mt. Pleasant *Home Journal* from August 1864 through July 1865. Twenty years later, Will submitted an article about the battle for the *National Tribune*, which may be similar to the account he refers to here. See Appendix A.

Aug	15	Firing from the picket pits has been severe all day, wounded or dead are brought in almost every night[.]
Aug	17"	"G" went on picket after dark. In the night fighting off to right , no sleep for us all night.
Aug	18"	Keen sharpshooting back and forth. During a demonstration 30 rounds fired. We lost no men.
Aug	19"	Several attempts on various parts of the line today[.] Seemed to be feeling to see if we were there. Finished the works and the batteries moved out.
Aug	20"	Moved up to the new line, and fixed up bunks[.] It rained nearly all night[.]

Picket Station near Atlanta (Library of Congress)

| Aug | 21" | Batteries kept it up. Sharpshooting active. We have head logs, with portholes for shooting. |

| Aug | 22^d | Rebel batteries active. One of 15" wounded.[27] |

| Aug | 23^d | I was on detail digging a sap in front of 1" Brig. last night.[28] 17" A.C. pickets were advanced[.] Went on picket after dark, could hear the rebel videtts cough, or step. |

| Aug | 24" | Very little firing going on today. New line of works being built in the rear. |

| Aug | 25" | Marching orders[.] No one knows just where to, at dark moved back to new line in rear. |

| Aug | 26" | Rebs woke up about 8 A.M. but soon found us[.] We evacuated our lines at 8 P.M. moving to right[.] Left 20 corps to hold new works. The rebs thought all were gone, and came out on a rush, they ran into a line armed with 16 shooters, they had not lost any 16 shooters! |

| Aug | 27" | Marched about 12 miles last night lay on arms. Started at 7 A.M. Marched 4 miles. |

| Aug | 28 | Marched about 6 miles struck the M & A. R.R. threw up works, then destroyed the track. Heating and bending the rails around trees.[29] |

---

[27] Three members of the Fifteenth Iowa were wounded on 23 August 1864. (Baker, *Report*, 1:732-763).

[28] A sap is a zigzag trench used to advance on enemy fortifications, typically about seven feet deep and eight feet wide (Garrison, *Civil War Usage*, 220; Shea and Winschel, *Vicksburg is the Key*, 155).

[29] Probably the Macon and Western Railroad (M.& W. R. R.), which ran through Clayton County.

Aug	29"	Laid in the shade and rested for the first time for over 70 days. Had some sweetpotatoes.
Aug	30"	Remained in camp till 8 P.M. We are rear guard Army of [the] Tenn. Report of capture of Mobile.
Aug	31"	Maneuvered around until 9 P.M.
Sept	1"	Fell in at 11 last night and moved to left[.] At 2 A.M. threw up pits, and remained until 2 P.M. then marched about 5 miles to right. There was heavy skirmishing, at dusk we were into position, and "G" went on picket, relieved later[.][30]
Sept	2^d	About 3 A.M. there was a lively noise and fireworks at Atlanta. The sky was full of bursting shells and flashes of fire.[31] We soon found they had evacuated and started South West after them[.] Tramped nearly all day, and threw up a line.
Sept	3^d	Laid in camp all day. Strengthened our lines.
Sept	4"	Still in same place near Lovejoy Station[.]
Sept	5"	Orders to march at 8 P.M. Mud worked up until it is halfleg deep, and nasty for night marching.
Sept	6"	Marched and stood all night. At daylight were about 5 miles from Lovejoy. Passed Jonesborough

---

[30] The "heavy skirmishing" was part of the Battle of Jonesborough.

[31] As the Confederates evacuated Atlanta, General Hood ordered the burning of military supplies and installations. In particular the reserve ordnance train of eighty-one cars was set on fire and caused "perhaps the greatest explosion of the American Civil War" (Russell S. Bonds, *War Like the Thunderbolt: the Battle and Burning of Atlanta* [Yardley, Pennsylvania: Westholme, 2009], 279-282).

and halted for breakfast. Moved along about 3 miles and camped. Cavalry skirmished all day.

Sept 7" Moved at 9 A.M. Marched about 8 miles and camped. All firing has stopped. It is so still that it seems strange.

Chapter XIII
"Started after Hood"
Last Marches and Mustering Out
September and October 1864

After the fall of Atlanta both the Confederate and Union forces spent a few weeks recovering from the campaign of the past few months. Sherman consolidated his victory by evacuating Atlanta's civilian population and arranging for keeping possession of that strategic rail center. It was also a time for planning the fall and winter campaigns, which included the famous March to the Sea. Confederate General Hood, inan attempt to draw Sherman out of Atlanta, and Georgia, struck out for Alabama and Tennessee in the beginning of October. Sherman followed with most of his army as far as Gaylesville, Alabama, which he reached by 20 October.[1]

Sept	8"	Marched at 8 A.M. soon heard the welcome sound of engine whistles camped in the rebel works, near a spring, built bunks. Received letters from Mother and Amelia.
Sept	9"	Moved across the Railroad and camped[.]
Sept	10"	Carried lumber two miles and built bunks desk &c. Knapsacks came to us, all right[.][2]
Sept	11	Co "G" on picket at 8 A.M. fine quiet day.
Sept	12	About midnight last night while I was vidette, a horseman in full rebel gray rode up to me from the

---

[1] Cox, *Atlanta*, 218, 239.

[2] Their knapsacks had been left at Huntsville, Alabama, in May (Fultz MS, 116).

South. He proved to be a scout belonging to 2^d Ills Cav.[3] Wrote to Mother Amelia and Robert.

Sept	13"	Had letters from Mother and Wade.
Sept	15	Regimental Inspection. Lasting nearly all day.
Sept	16"	Went into the city, found some thin lumber and boxed my knapsack.
Sept	17"	Celebrated my birthday by going on picket. A long train of women and children sent South, went by where we were stationed.
Sept	18"	It has rained nearly all day. I fixed up our gum blankets and kept fairly dry.
Sept	20	Started early for a tramp over the battle ground of July 22^d. Everything was just as it was then. I cut a cane at Bald Knob, and picked up a few mementos. It has been two months since the battle. Drew tents.
Sept	21"	On picket. Day fairly pleasant. Some rain during afternoon.
Sept	23^d	Came off picket at 8 A.M. Company drew clothing[.] Rained again.
Sept	25	This is a beautiful, sunny, quiet Sunday[.] Warm and everyway pleasant.
Sept	27"	On picket duty again. It seems like playing after the kind of life we have led lately.

---

[3] The only Illinois cavalry in the vicinity was Company G, Eleventh Illinois Cavalry under Captain Stephen S. Tripp, which served as the XVII Corps headquarters escort (*OR* 38, pt. 1, 109-110). It is more likely that Will means a scout from the Second Indiana Cavalry.

Sept 28"   I was up and down at a little brook taking a bath as reveille sounded.

Sept 30"   Fixed up a little and spent the greater part of the day in reading.

The Iowa Brigade left camp on 1 October heading toward Fairburn. They skirmished with the Confederates briefly and returned to camp 3 October.[4] Sherman learned on 2 October that Confederate General Hood and his army had crossed the Chattahoochee River. Leaving the XX Corps as a garrison at Atlanta, Sherman began pursuit of Hood with all the rest of his forces.[5]

Oct 4"   Started after Hood. Put in a hard day, after making 14 miles camped in old rebel works.[6]

Oct 5"   Marched at 7 A.M. leaving Marietta to our right, reached a line of works west of Kennesaw Mt and camped for the night.

Oct 6   We remained in camp all day. In the evening visited 17 A.C. Hdqrs, saw Courtney and others of 11".

Oct 7"   On the road at 9 A.M. marching west. Passed through Powder Springs at 5[.] A pretty little place. five miles beyond we camped in works built by the Johnies.

---

[4] *Downing's Civil War Diary*, 218-219; Fultz MS. 119.

[5] Casteel, *Decision in the West*, 552.

[6] Four miles west of Marietta, according to both Alex Downing and Mifflin Jennings. Jennings claims they marched 18 miles, while Fultz states it was 25 miles (Jennings, October 4th; *Downing's Civil War Diary*, 219; Fultz MS. 120).

Oct	8"	Started back at 6 A.M. by noon reached our camp of Oct 6, Making about 13 miles. The weather is cold and fine for marching.
Oct	9"	Marched at 6 A.M. moved North along the railroad., passed Kennesaw Mountain at 10. We halted a while and several of the boys walked to the summit, where they found a lake and a grand view of parts of three states. 7 miles.[7]
Oct	10"	Last night was cold but this morning is sunny and pleasant. The army is at work on the railroad. I built a shebang and washed[.]
Oct	11"	Broke camp at 2 A.M. going North on the Railroad. Passed Ackworth Station, and halted about a mile beyond for breakfast, soon off again, about noon reached Altoona.[8] It was 6 days after the battle, a lot of rebel wounded in tents, one a woman in mens clothes swore at me for looking into the tent. Crossed the Etowa river and camped[.]
Oct	12	Started at 7 A.M. passed through Cartersville. About 5 P.M. reached Kingston, beyond the town halted for supper and to receive our mail[.] Letters from Amelia, Robert, Wade and Campbell. Campbell and White came back to us.[9]
Oct	13"	Started at 7.30 last evening and kept it up till midnight before camping. I spent the balance of

---

[7] The Eleventh went into bivouac at Big Shanty (*Downing's Civil War Diary*, 220; Fultz MS, 121).

[8] Allatoona Pass is located in Bartow County, Georgia. The battle there took place on 5 October 1864.

[9] Hiram A. White. See Appendix B.

		the night trying to find some way to sleep with rheumatic hips. Six or seven miles.[10]
Oct	14"	Marched at 5 last evening arriving at (6 or 7 miles) Adairsville at 1 A.M. where at 3 we took train for Resaca, 15 miles arrived at 9 A.M. Moved to Northern part of town and took position.
Oct	15"	Moved from Resaca at 7 A.M. about 5 miles out overtook the rebs and after a brisk skirmish drove them into and through Snake Creek Gap. They were in rifle pits and had felled the timber. 15 miles[.][11]
Oct	16	Marched at 9 A.m. Some skirmishing ahead. We passed a rebel lieutenant and some of his men lying dead.
Oct	17"	Our papers for discharge were nearly done today, but Gen. Belknap would not allow them given out.[12] At dress parade the Non veterans of Co "G" stacked their guns, but all finally took them again except Winder and myself. I had some hot talk with Capt. Barr[.][13]

---

[10] Camp was within five miles of Rome, Georgia (*Downing's Civil War Diary*, 221).

[11] This skirmish was fought against Brantly's and Deas's brigades (report of Lt. Gen. Stephen D. Lee, *OR* 1:39 [pt. 1], 811).

[12] Brigadier General William Worth Belknap (1829-1890) was a lawyer and legislator from Keokuk, Iowa. Beginning the war as major in the Fifteenth Iowa Infantry, he rose to command of the Fourth Division of the XVII corps by the Atlanta Campaign (Warner, *Generals in Blue*, 29-30).

[13] The "hot talk" probably was over Will's abandonment of his rifle and accoutrements, the cost of which ($23.68) was deducted from his muster out pay (Compiled military service record, William L. Wade, Pvt., Co. G, 11 Ia. Inf., Civil War, RG 94, NA-Washington).

Oct	18"	Marched at 7 last evening over a small mountain for four miles and camped. At 8 A.M. took the Chattooga road, at 12.30 halted for dinner.[14] Marching is light work without any gun or accouterments. Camped near the Chattooga river.
Oct	19"	Marched through Summersville and Alpine following the Chattooga Valley South West. We camped about a mile beyond Alpine at the crossing of the Bridgeport road. 14 miles.[15]
Oct	20"	Started off at 7 A.M. in the advance. Found plenty of sweetpotatoes. Camped near Gaylesville, 10 miles.
Oct	21"	At 11 A.M. moved through Gaylesville about 4 miles and camped in a grove of pines.
Oct	22[d]	Were formally mustered out of service at 8 A.M. with orders to start North at 12 M. I took a good bath and after bidding all good bye, we marched to Corps Headquarters where we waited until 4 P.M. When we got off marched to and beyond Gaylesville about 3 miles and camped for the night. Made 6 miles.
Oct	23[d]	We marched through a good country, not stripped by foragers, found plenty of sweetpotatoes, lambs, and pigs. 24 miles.
Oct	24"	Marched to LaFayette for dinner.[16] The weather cool and bracing. Made 25 miles.

---

[14] At LaFayette (Fultz MS, 124).

[15] Near Chattoogaville on the state line (Jennings, October 19th; Fultz MS, 125).

[16] LaFayette is in Walker County, Georgia.

Lee and Gordon's Mill, Chickamauga (Editor's Collection)

Oct	25"	Left camp at daylight, marching North on Chattanooga road. In a short time came to the old Lee and Gordons Mill, and crossing a bridge we almost at once were upon the great Chic[k]amauga battlefield. The marks of the terrible conflict were still in evidence, trees torn by shot, and shell, graves of the thousands who fell and we found a skeleton of an unburied union Soldier lying where he fell over a year ago. We arrived at Chattanooga at 1 P.M. after tramping 15 miles. We camped near the Tennessee river, drew full rations[.]
Oct	26	We were promised transportation North at 2 P.M. but were disappointed. We thought there was some scheme in the matter and demanded our

		discharge and transportation papers, and at 6 P.M. were off for Louisville[.]
Oct	27"	Bowled along until 2 A.M. when we were delayed near Stevenson, by the failure of the Northern train.[17] Laid by all day, till nearly dark. When we moved on.
Oct	28"	Arrived in Nashville at 4 A.M. Put up at the soldiers Home took breakfast and dinner at 2 P.M.[18] Started for Louisville.
Oct	29"	Were paid off. I received pay as follows

Back Bounty	100.
Four months @ 13.	52.
Five months 18 ds at 16	89.60
Clothing allowance	25.06
	$266.96[19]

---

[17] Stephenson is located just to the east of Hillsboro, in Coffee County, Tennessee.

[18] The U.S. Sanitary Commission had by May 1864 established a Soldiers' Home in Nashville at the Planter's Hotel on Summer Street. It was evidently "a comfortable asylum to our war-worn heroes who often find it necessary to tarry here for a night or two on their way through the city; and are sure to receive, as they deserve, counsel, assistance, a warm welcome and ungrudging hospitality" ("Our Nashville Correspondence," *New York Times*, 4 July 1864).

[19] Will had not been paid since 31 December 1863 (Compiled military service record, William L. Wade, Pvt., Co. G, 11 Ia. Inf., Civil War, RG 94, NA-Washington).

Appendix A

The National Tribune (Washington, D.C.), 3 July 1884, p. 7, c. 4.

BALD KNOB.

The Part taken in the Fight by Crocker's Iowa Brigade.

TO THE EDITOR. Some time since there was quite a contention between comrades as to who did the fighting on Bald Knob, July 22, 1864. A comrade of the 20th Illinois maintained that it was his brigade. I could not say who tended shop from 12 m. until about 4 p.m., as Crocker's brigade had a picnic of their own further to the left, where they withstood repeated charges both in front and rear, and were compelled to change over first to one side and then to the other of their works. The fighting was so close that at one time a part of the 35th Alabama were on one side of the works and just the earthworks between us. The boys sustained their usual reputation and took in the 35th's colors and a number of Johnnies.[1] Crocker's brigade never had the reputation of being driven easily, and Hood's report shows that it was a terribly costly on this occasion. It was well toward evening when we reached the Knob, the last hundred yards being up an incline, perfectly smooth, and completely raked by the canister and rifle-balls of the enemy. Some declined to take such slim chances, and several officers and men of the 11th were captured only a few yards from the works. When I jumped over the works I found so many Iowa men (Crocker's) that I supposed we were running things. Lieut.-Col. Shedd, 20th Illinois,[2] was there, but surrounded by Iowa men, and on his left, Capt. Anderson, of Co. A, 11th Iowa,[3] was holding an embrasure where rebel guns had stood on

---

[1] The Forty-fifth Alabama's colors were captured by Edward Siberts of Comapny G. See Appendix B.

[2] Col. Warren Shedd commanded the Thirtieth Illinois Infantry at Atlanta (*Report of the Adjutant General of the State of Illinois*, 1:64).

[3] Capt. John W. Anderson (1836-), a native of Indiana from Fairport, Iowa (*Roster and Record*, 2:287).

the 20th, and was a host in himself – encouraging the men, loading guns, pointing out officers, and occasionally doing some rapid shooting himself. Just at this point a rebel officer was very conspicuous; he was always in the lead, cheering his men forward, and he urged them to go over the works, but the deadly fire of our rifles and their fast-thinning ranks outbalanced their leader's eloquence. Several of us presented our regards to this officer, but no one saw him fall; but the next morning he lay there with "His back to the field, his feet to the foe." During the flag of truce his men buried him, and gave his name as Capt. F. A. Bohn, Co. B, 3d battalion, C. S. A. About 6 p.m. cartridges were running low, and I distributed a box brought up by a signal lieutenant, whose name I should like to know, as he was a brave man. My impression is that I knew most of the men to whom I gave cartridges. The protracted fighting made some men reckless of danger. Some stopped just outside the works and fought until shot down by the charging rebels; some mounted the works and were killed in the act of aiming at the enemy. Our color-bearer, Serg't Buck, seemed utterly regardless of danger. He stood in exposed places and urged the men to stand by the colors. Once, when we were exposed to a perfect storm of lead and canister, he held the flag as high as he could, and sang, in a clear, steady voice, the "Star Spangled Banner." A few minutes later those colors, which no rebel ever touched, fell from his dying hands, but only for a second, when other strong, brave hands lifted them to the breeze.[4]

This battle, so far as the Iowa brigade was concerned, was as great a surprise as Shiloh, if not a greater, our first warning, almost, being a volley from the rear, while at Shiloh we marched about a mile, formed a line of battle, and received the enemy in front in good style. Yet such was the love of the Army of the Tennessee for its commander, McPherson, that to this day I have never heard a word of reproach from one of them. – W. L. WADE, Co. G., 11th Iowa, Salem, Ore.

---

[4] First sergeant John A. Buck (1842-1864), Co. K, was a native of Pennsylvania from Lisbon, Scott County, Iowa (*Roster and Record*, 2:281, 299).

Appendix B
Roster of Company G

This roster of Company G, Eleventh Iowa Infantry, contains all known members, exclusive of those who were discharged at the mustering in of the company on 15 October 1861. Those who were transferred to Company B on that date are included as they remained with the regiment. The sources for each soldier follow each entry. "Cemetery records" refers to information from the following sources: Find A Grave (http://www.findagrave.com); United States Department of Veterans Affairs (http://gravelocator.cem.va.gov); the Sons of Union Veterans of the Civil War Graves Registration Database (http://www.suvcwdb.org); or the Iowa WPA Graves Survey (http://iowawpagraves.org).

Abbe, Henry Leander. Born 1835 in Connecticut. Residence Mount Pleasant. Enlisted 12 September 1861, as Seventh Corporal. Mustered in 15 October 1861. Promoted Fifth Corporal 6 November 1861. Transferred to Invalid Corps 15 February 1864. Died 12 September 1874 in Henry County, Iowa. (*Roster and Record*, 2:289 [Henry Abby]; Henry L. Abbe, *Organization Index to Pension Files of Veterans who served between 1861 and 1900*; 1860 U.S. census, Henry Co., Iowa, Baltimore twp., Mt. Pleasant, p. 419, Jno B Abby; cemetery records.)

Alvey, James M. Born 13 August 1833 in Indiana. Residence Keosauqua, Van Buren County. Enlisted 23 September 1861. Mustered 15 October 1861. Wounded 6 April 1862, Shiloh, Tennessee. Promoted Second Corporal 17 April 1863. Discharged for disability 18 October 1864 at Davenport, Iowa. Died 3 June 1890 in Van Buren County. (*Roster and Record*, 2:290; James M. Alvey, *Organization Index to Pension Files of Veterans who served between 1861 and 1900;* cemetery records.)

Anderson, Joseph P. Born 1846 in Ohio. Residence New London, Henry County. Enlisted 5 October 1864. Mustered in 15 October 1864. Mustered out 2 June 1865 at Washington, D. C.

Died 1905 in California. (*Roster and Record*, 2:290; Joseph P. Anderson, *Organization Index to Pension Files of Veterans who served between 1861 and 1900;* cemetery records.)

Barr, David H. Born 14 July 1838 in Alleghany County, Pennsylvania. Residence Mount Pleasant. Enlisted 9 September 1861. Mustered in 15 October 1861. Discharged for disability 21 October 1862 at the hospital at Keokuk, Iowa. Died 25 April 1913 at Wayland, Henry County.(*Roster and Record*, 2:296; Baker, *Report of the Adjutant General*, 424; David H. Barr, *Organization Index to Pension Files of Veterans who served between 1861 and 1900*; 1860 U.S. census, Henry Co., Iowa, Center twp., Mt. Pleasant, p. 131, David Barr; *Biographical Review of Henry County, Iowa* [Chicago: Hobart Publishing, 1906], 109.)

Barr, George W. F. Born 8 March 1836 in Pennsylvania. Residence Mount Pleasant. Had previously served in the First Iowa Infantry. Appointed Second Lieutenant and mustered in 15 October 1861. Promoted First Lieutenant 13 June 1862; Captain 25 August 1862. Taken prisoner 22 July 1864, Atlanta, Georgia. Returned from prison 1 October 1864. Mustered out 26 October 1864 at Gaylesville, Alabama. Died 3 October 1912 at Hastings, Adams County, Nebraska. (1860 Marion township, Henry Co., Mt. Pleasant post office, Iowa) (*Roster and Record*, 2:296; Baker, *Report of the Adjutant General*, 424; George W. Barr, *Organization Index to Pension Files of Veterans who served between 1861 and 1900*, cemetery records.)

Barr, John. Born 7 March 1826 in Pennsylvania. Residence Mount Pleasant. Enlisted and mustered in 19 October 1861. Taken prisoner 22 July 1864 near Atlanta, Georgia. Mustered out 15 July 1865 at Clinton, Iowa. Died 30 September 1898 in Henry County, Iowa. (*Roster and Record*, 2:296; 1860 U.S. census, Henry Co., Iowa, Wayne twp., p. 471, A. Barr; cemetery records.)

Beeler, John W. Born about 1841 in Pennsylvania. Residence Mount Pleasant. Enlisted 25 September 1861. Mustered 15 October 1861. Re-enlisted and re-mustered 1 January 1864. Wounded severely and taken prisoner 22 July 1864, near Atlanta,

Georgia. Died 17 January 1865, Annapolis, Maryland. Buried in Annapolis National Cemetery, Section B, Site 474 (National Cem. Records have 9 January 1865). *(Roster and Record*, 2:296; 1860 U.S. census, Henry Co., Iowa, Marion twp., Mt. Pleasant p. o., p. 317, Saml Beeler; cemetery records.)

Beeson, Henry Martin. Born 7 December 1839 in Ohio. Residence Albion, Marshall County. Enlisted 17 September 1861. Mustered in 25 October 1861. Enlisted and mustered 18 November 1861 in Company B, Second Iowa Cavalry. Promoted bugler. Discharged 18 November 1864 at Memphis, Tennessee. Died 20 August 1923 in Marshall County, Iowa. (*Roster and Record*, 2:296, 4:248; Henry M. Beeson, *General Index to Pension Files of Veterans, 1861-1934;* cemetery records.)

Bevins, John W. Born about 1835 in Indiana. Residence Millersburg, Iowa County. Enlisted 20 September 1861. Mustered in and transferred to Company B 15 October 1861. Died of fever 4 June 1862 at Monterey, Tennessee. (*Roster and Record*, 2:292, 296.)

Black, William. Born about 1836 in Ireland. Residence Keosauqua, Van Buren County. Enlisted 14 September 1861. Mustered in 15 October 1861. Killed in battle 6 April 1862 at Shiloh, Tennessee. (*Roster and Record*, 2:297; Baker, *Report of the Adjutant General*, 425.)

Bledsoe, Benjamin H. Born about 1841 in Indiana. Residence Mount Pleasant. Enlisted 25 September 1861. Mustered in 15 October 1861. Transferred to Invalid Corps 15 March 1864. (*Roster and Record*, 2:297; 1860 U.S. census, Louisa County, Iowa, Columbus City, p. 839, William J Pletsoe.)

Bolean, William L. Born about 1834 in Ohio. Residence Port Louisa, Louisa County. Enlisted 9 October 1861. Mustered in 15 October 1861. Mustered out 17 October 1864 at Galesville, Alabama. Died in Johnson County, Missouri. (*Roster and Record*, 2:297; William L. Bolean, *Organization Index to Pension Files of Veterans who served between 1861 and 1900;* cemetery records.)

Bower, Benjamin F. Born 17 August 1835 in Pennsylvania. Residence Mount Pleasant. Enlisted 9 September 1861, as Second Corporal. Mustered in 15 October 1861. Promoted First Corporal 6 November 1861. Re-enlisted and re-mustered 1 January 1864. Taken prisoner 22 July 1864, near Atlanta, Georgia. Promoted Fourth Sergeant 1 January 1865. Mustered out 15 July 1865 at Louisville, Kentucky. Died 15 April 1902 in Jefferson County, Iowa. (*Roster and Record*, 2:297 [Benjamin F. Bowen,]; Benjamin F. Bower, *Organization Index to Pension Files of Veterans who served between 1861 and 1900;* cemetery records.)

Campbell, Archibald S. Born 28 December 1845 in Iowa. Residence Mount Pleasant. Enlisted 10 September 1861. Mustered in 15 October 1861. Re-enlisted and re-mustered 1 January 1864. Wounded in left hand slightly 22 July 1864, near Atlanta, Georgia. Mustered out 15 July 1865, Louisville, Kentucky. Died 15 April 1886 in Doniphan County, Kansas. (*Roster and Record*, 2:305; Archibald S. Campbell, *Organization Index to Pension Files of Veterans who served between 1861 and 1900;* cemetery records.)

Cogswell, John H. Born about 1843 in Indiana. Residence Davenport, Scott County. Enlisted and mustered in 23 September 1864. Mustered out 2 June 1865 at Washington, D. C. Died 2 February 1923 at Bradford, Franklin County, Iowa. (*Roster and Record*, 2:305 [John H. Coggswell]; John H. Cogswell, *Organization Index to Pension Files of Veterans who served between 1861 and 1900.*)

Conner, Oscar H. Born 1 January 1842 in Ohio. Residence Mount Pleasant. Enlisted 17 September 1861. Mustered in 15 October 1861. Wounded in right leg slightly 22 July 1864 near Atlanta, Georgia. Mustered out 17 October 1864. Died 9 May 1905 in Dallas County, Iowa. (*Roster and Record*, 2:305; Oscar H. Conner, *Organization Index to Pension Files of Veterans who served between 1861 and 1900;* cemetery records.)

Conway, Lloyd N. Born 20 May 1842 in Ohio. Residence Le Grand, Marshall County. Enlisted 28 September 1861. Mustered in and transferred to Company B 15 October 1861. Wounded in left arm severely 22 July 1864, near Atlanta, Georgia. Mustered out 18 October 1864, Davenport, Iowa. Died 9 August 1906 in Madison County, Iowa. (*Roster and Record*, 2:305; Lloyd N. Conway, *Organization Index to Pension Files of Veterans who served between 1861 and 1900;* cemetery records.)

Courtney, Joseph L. Born 13 July 1835 in Ohio. Residence Mount Pleasant. Enlisted 9 September 1861, as Second Sergeant. Mustered in 15 October 1861. Promoted Quartermaster Sergeant 6 November 1861. Re-enlisted and re-mustered 1 January 1864. Taken prisoner 22 July 1864 near Atlanta, Georgia. Mustered out 21 June 1865 at Davenport, Iowa. Died 22 February 1912 in Beaver County, Pennsylvania. (*Roster and Record*, 2:305; cemetery records.)

Cozier, Henry. Born 25 December 1840 in Ohio. Residence Mount Pleasant. Enlisted 12 September 1861. Mustered in 15 October 1861. Transferred to Mississippi Marine Brigade 6 April 1863. Died 19 October 1885 in Henry County, Iowa. (*Roster and Record*, 2:306; cemetery records.)

Crooks, Lawson. Born about 1841 in Ohio. Residence Keosauqua, Van Buren County. Enlisted 28 September 1861. Mustered in 15 October 1861. Transferred to Elliott's Marine Brigade 10 April 1863. (*Roster and Record*, 2:306; 1860 U.S. census, Van Buren Co., Iowa, Des Moines twp., p. 192, John M Crooks.)

Dailey, Caleb. Born 4 January 1845 in Ohio. Residence Mount Pleasant. Enlisted 16 September 1861. Mustered in 15 October 1861. Promoted Fifth Corporal 13 March 1864. Missing in action 22 July 1864 near Atlanta, Georgia. Promoted Third Corporal 9 November 1864; Second Corporal 1 January 1865. Mustered out 15 June 1865 at Davenport, Iowa. Died 2 July 1900 in Henry County, Iowa. (*Roster and Record*, 2:313; Caleb Dailey, *Organization Index to Pension Files of Veterans who served between 1861 and 1900*; 1860 U.S. census, Henry Co., Iowa, New London, p. 268, F F Dailey; cemetery records.)

Dailey, Francis M. Born about 1835. Residence Mount Pleasant, nativity Ohio. Enlisted Sept. 16, 1861. Mustered Oct. 15, 1861. Re-enlisted and re-mustered Jan. 1, 1864. Mustered out July 15, 1865, Louisville, Ky. (*Roster and Record*, 2:313; 1860 U.S. census, Henry Co., Iowa, New London, p. 268, F M Dailey; cemetery records.)

Dailey, Joseph T. Born about 1841 in Ohio. Residence Mount Pleasant. Enlisted 25 September 1861. Mustered in 15 October 1861. Re-enlisted and re-mustered 1 January 1864. Wounded slightly 19 and 23 August 1864 near Atlanta, Georgia. Mustered out 15 July 1865 at Louisville, Kentucky. Died 10 December 1910 at DuBois, Pawnee County, Nebraska. (*Roster and Record*, 2:313; Joseph T. Dailey, *Organization Index to Pension Files of Veterans who served between 1861 and 1900*; 1860 U.S. census, Henry Co., Iowa, New London, p. 268, F F Dailey; cemetery records.)

Davis, Amos C. Born 23 March 1836 in Indiana. Residence Mount Pleasant. Enlisted 16 September 1861. Mustered in 15 October 1861. Promoted Hospital Steward. Appointed Assistant Surgeon of Eighth Louisiana Volunteers (48 U.S. Colored Infantry) 6 June 1863. Promoted Surgeon 9 March 1864. Resigned 11 February 1865. Died 24 April 1915 at Topeka, Shawnee County, Kansas. (*Roster and Record*, 2:313; Amos C. Davis, *Organization Index to Pension Files of Veterans who served between 1861 and 1900;* Compiled military service record, Amos C. Davis, Surgeon, 48 U.S. Colored Inf., Civil War, RG 94, NA-Washington; cemetery records.)

Delong, Bernard A. Born 30 October 1848 in Ohio. Residence New London, Henry County. Enlisted and mustered in 5 October 1864. Mustered out 15 July 1865 at Louisville, Kentucky. Died 4 July 1926 at North Loup, Valley County, Nebraska. (*Roster and Record*, 2:313; Bernard De Long, *Organization Index to Pension Files of Veterans who served between 1861 and 1900*; cemetery records.)

Doudney, John. Born about 1845 in New Jersey. Residence Wilton, Muscatine County. Enlisted and mustered in 5 October 1864. Mustered out 15 July 1865, Louisville, Kentucky. Died 15 January 1933 at Wyoming, Jones County, Iowa. (*Roster and Record*, 2:314; John Doudney, *Organization Index to Pension Files of Veterans who served between 1861 and 1900*.)

Dunning, Robert. Born 14 May 1843 in Kentucky. Residence Davenport, Scott County. Enlisted and mustered in 3 September 1862. Missing in action 22 July 1864 near Atlanta, Georgia. Mustered out 2 June 1865, Washington, D. C. Died 1 May 1915 in Wapello County, Iowa. (*Roster and Record*, 2:314 [Robert Dunning]; Robert Duning, *Organization Index to Pension Files of Veterans who served between 1861 and 1900;* cemetery records.)

Ellenbarger, John B. Born 4 August 1823 in Indiana. Residence Henry County. Enlisted and mustered in 5 September 1862. Mustered out 2 June 1865, Washington, D, C. Died 15 October 1908 in Jefferson County, Iowa. (*Roster and Record*, 2:318 [John Ellenbarger]; John Ellenberger, *Organization Index to Pension Files of Veterans who served between 1861 and 1900*; Iowa death certificate no. 43 [FHL 1750236].)

Flory, Francis M. Born about 1845 in Ohio. Residence Mount Pleasant. Enlisted 11 September 1861. Mustered in 15 October 1861. Re-enlisted and re-mustered 1 January 1864. Killed in battle 22 July 1864, near Atlanta, Georgia. Buried in Marietta National Cemetery. Section E, Grave 243. (*Roster and Record*, 2:322; 1860 U.S. census, Henry Co., Iowa, Mt. Pleasant, p. 114, G W Flory.)

Force, Franklin. Born about 1840 in Crawford County, Pennsylvania. Residence Mount Pleasant. Enlisted 16 September 1861. Mustered in 15 October 1861. Promoted Second Corporal 1 July 1862; Third Sergeant 17 April 1863. Discharged 16 December 1863, for promotion to Twelfth Louisiana Colored Volunteers. Adjutant of Fiftieth U. S. Colored Infantry. Died 22 May 1902 In Burt County, Nebraska. (*Roster and Record*, 2:322; Baker, *Report of the Adjutant General*, 425; Compiled military service record, Franklin Force, Adjutant, 50 U.S. Colored Inf.,

Civil War, RG 94, NA-Washington; Franklin Force, *Organization Index to Pension Files of Veterans who served between 1861 and 1900*; cemetery records.)

Foster, Samuel. Born about 1842 in Ohio. Residence Mount Pleasant. Enlisted 17 September 1861, as First Corporal. Mustered in 15 October 1861. Promoted Second Sergeant 6 November 1861; First Sergeant 1 July 1862; Second Lieutenant 29 February 1863; Captain 27 October 1864. Mustered out 15 July 1865 at, Louisville, Kentucky. Died 3 August 1886 in Kidder County, North Dakota. (*Roster and Record*, 2:322; Baker, *Report of the Adjutant General*, 424; Samuel Foster, *Organization Index to Pension Files of Veterans who served between 1861 and 1900*; 1860 U.S. census, Henry Co., Iowa, Scott twp., Winfield p. o., p. 448, Saml Foster; cemetery records.)

Gaskill, Elis. Born about 1842 in Iowa. Residence Mount Pleasant. Enlisted 25 September 1861. Mustered in 15 October 1861. Died 1 August 1862 at Corinth, Mississippi. (*Roster and Record*, 2:326; Baker, *Report of the Adjutant General*, 425; *Report of Brig.-Gen. Nathaniel B. Baker, Adjutant General...*, Vol. 1 [Des Moines, 1867], 639.)

Gilmore, Isaac N. Born 17 August 1847 in Ohio. Residence Banner Valley. Enlisted and mustered in 8 October 1864. Mustered out 15 July 1865, Louisville, Kentucky. Died 13 December 1921 at Marshalltown, Marshall County, Iowa. (*Roster and Record*, 2:327; Isaac N. Gilmore, *Organization Index to Pension Files of Veterans who served between 1861 and 1900*; cemetery records.)

Haltom, John J. Born about 1842 in Indiana. Residence Panora, Guthrie County, Iowa. Enlisted and mustered in 27 September 1864. Mustered out 2 June 1865, Washington, D C. Died 1 January 1919 at Panora, Guthrie County, Iowa. (*Roster and Record*, 2:333 [John J. Hatton]; John J. Haltom, *Organization Index to Pension Files of Veterans who served between 1861 and 1900*; 1860 U.S. census, Guthrie Co., Iowa, Elijah Haltom.)

Hanson, Arthur J. Born 20 July 1840 in Kentucky. Residence Germantown. Enlisted 18 September 1861. Mustered in and transferred to Company B 15 October 1861. Promoted First Sergeant 11 November 1863. Re-enlisted and re-mustered 1 January 1864. Promoted First Lieutenant 28 October 1864. Resigned 3 June 1865, Washington, D. C. Died 26 September 1896 in Madison County, Kentucky. (*Roster and Record*, 2:329, 333; cemetery records.)

Hauser, David. Born about 1834 in Indiana. Residence Marshall County. Enlisted 21 September 1861. Mustered and transferred to Company B 15 October 1861. Died of measles 30 December 1861, Jefferson City, Missouri. (*Roster and Record*, 2:329, 333.)

Heald, William. Born about 1839 in England. Residence Mount Pleasant. Enlisted 9 September 1861. Mustered in 15 October 1861. Promoted Second Sergeant. Re-enlisted and re-mustered 1 January 1864. Killed 22 July 1864, near Atlanta, Georgia. (*Roster and Record*, 2:333; 1860 U.S. census, Henry Co., Iowa, Center twp., Mt. Pleasant p. o., p. 146, N Heald.)

Hickok, Francis M. Born about 1845 in Ohio. Residence Mount Pleasant. Enlisted 12 September 1861. Mustered in 15 October 1861. Discharged for disability 6 May 1862 at St. Louis, Missouri. (*Roster and Record*, 2:334; 1860 U.S. census, Jefferson Co., Iowa, Round Prairie twp., Glasgow p. o., p. 179, Francis Hickcox.)

Hobert, Mortimer. Born about 1841 in New York. Residence Mount Pleasant. Enlisted 17 September 1861. Mustered in 15 October 1861. Killed in battle 6 April 1862 at Shiloh, Tennessee. (*Roster and Record, 2:334*; Baker, *Report of the Adjutant General*, 425; 1860 U.S. census, Henry Co., Iowa, Scott twp., Winfield p. o., p. 461, Wm Hobert.)

Holloway, Harrison. Born about 1837 in Ohio. Residence Mount Pleasant. Enlisted 20 September 1861. Mustered in 15 October 1861. Promoted Eighth Corporal 6 November 1861; Fifth Sergeant 1 June 1862. Re-enlisted and re-mustered 1 January 1864. Promoted Third Sergeant 29 September 1864; First Sergeant 1

January 1865. Mustered out 15 July 1865, Louisville, Kentucky. Died 27 November 1902 at Dayton, Ohio. (*Roster and Record*, 2:334; Baker, *Report of the Adjutant General*, 424; Harrison Holloway, *Organization Index to Pension Files of Veterans who served between 1861 and 1900*.)

Hudson, Andrew J. Born about 1840 in Ohio. Residence Mount Pleasant. Enlisted and mustered in 18 October 1861 in Company H. Transferred to Company G 1 January 1862. Re-enlisted and re-mustered Jan. 1, 1864. Killed in battle July 21, 1864, near Atlanta, Georgia. Buried in National Cemetery, Marietta, Georgia, Section E, grave 582. (*Roster and Record*, 2:334, 335; 1860 U.S. census, Polk Co., Iowa, Camp twp., p. 255, Enoch Hudson.)

Hull, Clinton Telemachus. Born 12 December 1842 at Ellison, Warren County, Illinois. Residence Mount Pleasant. Enlisted and mustered in 19 October 1861. Re-enlisted and re-mustered 1 January 1864. Taken prisoner 22 July 1864, near Atlanta, Georgia. Promoted Fifth Corporal 1 January 1865. Mustered out 15 July 1865, Louisville, Kentucky. Died 16 May 1910 at San Francisco, California. Buried in National Cemetery, San Francisco, California, Section NAWS, Grave 1507. (*Roster and Record*, 2:334; Clinton T. Hull, *Organization Index to Pension Files of Veterans who served between 1861 and 1900;* cemetery records; *Addresses delivered before the California Society of the Sons of the American Revolution; biographical sketches by Thomas Allen Perkins* [San Francisco, Calif.: The Society, 1913], 105-106.)

Hummell, George. Born 30 July 1847 in Iowa. Residence Center Township, Henry County. Enlisted and mustered in 28 March 1864. Wounded in right arm severely 22 July 1864, near Atlanta, Georgia. Died of wounds 11 September 1864 at Rome, Georgia. Buried in Marietta National Cemetery, Section C, Site 1487. (*Roster and Record*, 2:334; cemetery records.)

Hummell, William. Born 18 May 1844 at Mount Pleasant, Henry County, Iowa. Attended Howe's Academy. Enlisted 14 September 1861. Mustered in 15 October 1861. Re-enlisted and re-mustered 1 January 1864. Taken prisoner 22 July 1864, near Atlanta, Georgia.

Andersonville. Paroled December 1864. Mustered out 15 July 1865, Louisville, Kentucky. Died 14 February 1929 at Burlington, Des Moines County, Iowa. (*Roster and Record*, 2:334; *History of Des Moines County, Iowa* [Chicago: Western Historical Co., 1879], 643; William Hummell, *Organization Index to Pension Files of Veterans who served between 1861 and 1900.*)

Kauffman, John Wesley. Born 5 January 1844 in Ohio. Residence Mount Pleasant. Enlisted 11 September 1861, as Third Sergeant. Mustered in 15 October 1861. Discharged for disability 15 April 1863. Died 25 May 1904 at St. Louis, Missouri. (*Roster and Record*, 2:342; Baker, *Report of the Adjutant General*, 424; City of St. Louis [Missouri] Health Department death certificate no. 10572 [1904], John Wesley Kauffman.)

Kendell, Jesse. Born about 1840 in Ohio. Residence Mount Pleasant. Enlisted 11 September 1861. Mustered in 15 October 1861. Re-enlisted and re-mustered 1 January 1864. Taken prisoner 22 July 1864, near Atlanta, Georgia. (*Roster and Record*, 2:343.)

Kennedy, Daniel. Born about 1836 in Ireland. Residence Mount Pleasant. Enlisted 4 September 1861. Mustered in 15 October 1861. Re-enlisted and re-mustered 1 January 1864. Mustered out 15 July 1865 at Louisville, Kentucky. Died 1894 in Iowa. (*Roster and Record*, 2:343; cemetery records.)

Kilbourn, Charles. Born 3 August 1838 in Iowa. Residence Mount Pleasant. Enlisted 13 September 1861. Mustered in 15 October 1861. Re-enlisted and re-mustered 1 January 1864. Wounded in right arm severely 22 July 1864 near Atlanta, Georgia. Discharged 1 February 1865 at Keokuk, Iowa. Died 22 April 1896 in Henry County, Iowa. (*Roster and Record*, 2:343.)

Kingsbury, Joseph J. Born 30 January 1843 in Indiana. Residence Mount Pleasant. Enlisted 16 September 1861. Mustered in 15 October 1861. Discharged for disability 31 January 1862 at Fulton, Missouri. Died 16 January 1913 in Oswego, Labette County, Kansas. (*Roster and Record*, 2:343; Joseph J. Kingsbury,

Organization Index to Pension Files of Veterans who served between 1861 and 1900; cemetery records.)

Kingsbury, Madison M. Born 12 October 1839 in Franklin County, Indiana. Residence Mount Pleasant. Enlisted 16 September 1861, as Wagoner. Mustered in 15 October 1861. Transferred to Mississippi Marine Brigade 6 April 1863. Became Captain of Company F, Forty-sixth U. S. Colored Troops. Died 13 August 1920 at Oswego, Labette County, Kansas. (*Roster and Record,* 2:343; Baker, *Report of the Adjutant General,* 424; Madison M. Kingsbury, *Organization Index to Pension Files of Veterans who served between 1861 and 1900*; Record and Roster, 343; Nelson Case, ed., *History of Labette County, Kansas and Representative Citizens* [Chicago: Biographical Publishing Co., 1901], 437-438.)

Krudwig, Herman. Born about 1844 in Germany. Residence Sioux City, Woodbury County. Enlisted and mustered in 4 October 1864. Mustered out 15 July 1865, Louisville, Kentucky. Died 28 November 1903 at Kansas City, Jackson County, Missouri. Buried in Leavenworth National Cemetery, Section 17, Row 12, Site 10. (*Roster and Record,* 2:342 [Herman Kanwig]; Herman Krudwig, *Organization Index to Pension Files of Veterans who served between 1861 and 1900*; cemetery records.)

Laughridge, Isaac. Born about 1845 in Ireland. Residence Agency Township, Wapello County. Enlisted and mustered in 12 October 1864. Mustered out 15 July 1865, Louisville, Kentucky. Died 11 March 1909 at Wasson, Saline County, Illlinois. (*Roster and Record,* 2:348; Isaac Laughridge, *Organization Index to Pension Files of Veterans who served between 1861 and 1900.*)

Lehew, Robert Milton. Born 6 February 1845 in Ohio. Residence Mount Pleasant. Enlisted and mustered in 1 January 1864. Wounded 17 June 1864. Mustered out 15 July 1865 at Louisville, Kentucky. Died 28 December 1928 at San Diego, California. (*Roster and Record,* 2:348; Robert M. Lehew, *Organization Index to Pension Files of Veterans who served between 1861 and 1900.*)

Lehew, Thomas H. Born about 1842 in Ohio. Residence Mount Pleasant. Enlisted 20 September 1861. Mustered in 15 October 1861. Re-enlisted and re-mustered 1 January 1864. Mustered out 15 July 1865 at Louisville, Kentucky. Died 10 December 1882 in Henry County, Iowa. (*Roster and Record*, 2:348; Thomas H. Lehew, *General Index to Pension Files 1861-1934*; cemetery records)

Lehew, William Fletcher Born 1 December 1824 in Muskingum County, Ohio. Residence Mount Pleasant. Enlisted 15 September 1861. Appointed First Lieutenant and mustered in 15 October 1861. Resigned 12 June 1862 at Corinth, Mississippi. Died 17 November 1892 at Baldwin, Douglas County, Kansas. (*Roster and Record*, 2:348; cemetery records.)

Lewis, Ephraim. Born 1 May 1832 in Pennsylvania. Residence Mount Pleasant. Enlisted 11 September 1861. Mustered in 15 October 1861. Mustered out 17 October 1864 at Gaylesville, Alabama. Died 23 December 1906 in Jefferson County, Nebraska. (*Roster and Record*, 2:348; Ephraim Lewis, *Organization Index to Pension Files of Veterans who served between 1861 and 1900;* cemetery records) records.)

Linkins, William C. Born about 1842 in Ohio. Residence Mount Pleasant. Enlisted 25 September 1861. Mustered in 15 October 1861. Re-enlisted and re-mustered 1 January 1864. Mustered out 15 July 1865 at Louisville, Kentucky. Died 2 November 1918 at New London, Henry County, Iowa. (*Roster and Record*, 2:348; William C. Linkins, *Organization Index to Pension Files of Veterans who served between 1861 and 1900.*)

Lockwood, Edwin J. Born 30 September 1839 in Delaware. Residence Port Louisa, Louisa County. Enlisted 9 October 1861, as Eighth Corporal. Mustered in 15 October 1861. Promoted Seventh Corporal 6 November 1861. First Sergeant 17 April 1863. Re-enlisted and re-mustered 1 January 1864. Promoted First Lieutenant 17 December 1864. Resigned 28 June 1865. Died 11 June 1893 in Union County, Iowa. (*Roster and Record*, 2:348; cemetery records.)

Lowry, Ambrose. Born 11 March 1843 in Athens County, Ohio. Residence Mount Pleasant. Enlisted 11 September 1861. Mustered in 15 October 1861. Died 6 February 1863, Keokuk, Iowa. Buried in Keokuk National Cemetery, Section A, Site 448. (*Roster and Record*, 2:349; Baker, *Report of the Adjutant General*, 425; *Roster and Record*, 349; *Report of Brig.-Gen. Nathaniel B. Baker*, 639.)

McCafferty, George. Born about 1840 in Ohio. Residence Mount Pleasant. Enlisted 25 September 1861. Mustered in 15 October 1861. Taken prisoner 22 July 1864 near Atlanta, Georgia. Died 8 March 1865. Buried in Wilmington National Cemetery, North Carolina. Section 3, Site 2024. (*Roster and Record*, 2:353.)

McClellan, James W. Born about 1835 in Ohio. Residence Mount Pleasant. Enlisted 25 September 1861. Mustered in 15 October 1861. Discharged for disability 21 January 1862 at Jefferson City, Missouri. (*Roster and Record*, 2:353.)

McCormick, John. Born about 1824 in Virginia. Residence Jasper County. Enlisted and mustered in 23 September 1864. Died 11 November 1864 at Chattanooga, Tennessee. Buried in Chattanooga National Cemetery. Section G, Site 8264. (*Roster and Record*, 2:354.)

McCune, Jeremiah. Born about 1828 in Indiana. Residence Wayne Township. Enlisted and mustered in 15 December 1863. Mustered out 15 July 1865 at Louisville, Kentucky. Died 5 January 1908 in Marshall County, Iowa. (*Roster and Record*, 2:354; cemetery records.)

McFarland, Samuel. Born 18 August 1824 in Washington County, Pennsylvania. Residence Mount Pleasant. Appointed Captain and mustered in 15 October 1861. Promoted Lieutenant Colonel of Nineteenth Infantry 2 August 1862. Discharged for promotion 10 September 1862. Mustered in 2 October 1862. Killed in action 7 December 1862 at Prairie Grove, Arkansas. (*Roster and Record*, 2:354; A.A. Stuart, *Iowa Colonels and Regiments* [Des Moines: Mills, 1865], 353; Nathaniel B. Baker,

Report of the Adjutant General and Acting Quartermaster General of Iowa [Des Moines: 1868], 424; *History of Henry County, Iowa* [Chicago: Western Historical Co., 1879], 665-667.)

McGavic, James. Born about 1832 in Virginia. Residence Mount Pleasant. Enlisted 12 September 1861. Mustered in 15 October 1861. Promoted Sixth Corporal. Died of chronic diarrhea 26 July 1863 at Black River Bridge, Mississippi. (*Roster and Record*, 2:354.)

McNeeley, George. Born 16 October 1840 in Highland County, Ohio. Residence Mount Pleasant. Enlisted 14 September 1861, as Fifth Corporal. Mustered in 15 October 1861. Promoted Fourth Sergeant 1 June 1862. Re-enlisted and re-mustered 1 January 1864. Taken prisoner 22 July 1864 near Atlanta, Georgia. Promoted Second Sergeant 29 September 1864. Mustered out 15 June 1865 at Davenport, Iowa. Died 19 January 1906 at Russell, Lucas County, Iowa. (*Roster and Record*, 2:354; George McNeeley obituary, *Chariton* [Iowa] *Leader*, 25 January 1906.)

Mahaffey, Alfred B. Born 13 February 1841 in Ohio. Residence Mount Pleasant. Enlisted 12 September 1861. Mustered in 15 October 1861. Discharged for disability 25 November 1862 at Grand Junction, Tennessee. Died 22 November 1902 in Denton County, Texas. (*Roster and Record*, 2:361; Alfred B. Mahaffey, *Organization Index to Pension Files of Veterans who served between 1861 and 1900;* cemetery records.)

Manlove, John H. Born about 1840 in Ohio. Residence Winfield, Henry County. Enlisted 9 October 1861. Mustered in 15 October 1861. Mustered out 17 October 1864 at Gaylesville, Alabama. Died 31 October 1864. Buried in Henry County, Iowa. (*Roster and Record*, 2:361; cemetery records.)

Manlove, Walter B. Brother of John H. Manlove. Born about 1843 in Ohio. Residence Winfield, Henry County. Enlisted 9 October 1861. Mustered in 15 October 1861. Discharged for disability 25 November 1862. (*Roster and Record*, 2:361; 1860

U.S. census, Henry Co., Iowa, pop. sch., Scott twp., Winfield p. o., p. 447, W. C. Manlove.)

Marriott, David. Born 13 December 1838 in Ohio. Residence Keosauqua, Van Buren County. Enlisted 28 September 1861. Mustered in 15 October 1861. Mustered out 17 October 1864 at Gaylesville, Alabama. Died 26 September 1910 in Van Buren County, Iowa. (*Roster and Record*, 2:362 [David Merialt]; David Marriott, *Organization Index to Pension Files of Veterans who served between 1861 and 1900;* cemetery records.)

Mars, Charles P. Born about 1845 in Iowa. Residence Davenport, Scott County. Enlisted and mustered in 8 October 1864. Mustered out 15 July 1865, Louisville, Kentucky. Died 26 February 1921 at San Diego, California. (*Roster and Record*, 2:361; Charles P. Mars, *Organization Index to Pension Files of Veterans who served between 1861 and 1900.*)

Martin, James L. Born 6 May 1833 in Indiana. Residence Marshall County. Enlisted 21 September 1861. Mustered in and transferred to Company B 15 October 1861. Promoted Eighth Corporal 8 April 1862; Fifth Corporal 15 August 1862; Fifth Sergeant 20 Feb 1863; Fourth Sergeant 19 April 1863; Third Sergeant 11 November 1863. Taken prisoner 22 July 1864, near Atlanta, Georgia. Mustered out 31 January 1865 at Clinton, Iowa. Died 26 February 1917 at Humansville, Polk County, Missouri. (*Roster and Record*, 2:361; James L. Martin, *Organization Index to Pension Files of Veterans who served between 1861 and 1900; Polk County, Missour death certificate no. 7176, James L. Martin [1917], Missouri State Board of Health.*)

Martin, Sheridan S. Born about 1839 in Ohio. Residence Wayne Township. Enlisted 15 December 1863. Mustered in 5 January 1864. Taken prisoner 22 July 1864, near Atlanta, Georgia. Died 19 Sept 1864, Andersonville, Georgia. Buried in Andersonville National Cemetery, Grave 9274. (*Roster and Record*, 2:361.)

Mead, Michael. Born about 1838 in New York. Residence Mount Pleasant. Enlisted 12 September 1861, as Third Corporal.

Mustered in 15 October 1861. Promoted Second Corporal 6 November 1861. Discharged for disability 27 August 1862. (*Roster and Record*, 2:362; 1860 U.S. census, Henry Co., Iowa, Marion twp., Mt. Pleasant p. o., p. 343, Mike Mead.)

Miller, George F. Born about 1827 in Pennsylvania. Residence Mount Pleasant. Enlisted 9 September, 1861. Mustered 15 October, 1861. Re-enlisted and re-mustered 1 January 1864. Mustered out 15 July 1865 at Louisville, Kentucky. (*Roster and Record*, 2:362.)

Miller, Madison J. Born about 1841 in Ohio. Residence Winfield, Henry County. Enlisted 17 September 1861. Mustered in 15 October 1861. Promoted Fourth Corporal. Killed in battle 22 July 1864 near Atlanta, Georgia. Buried in Marietta National Cemetery. Section E, Site 5783. (*Roster and Record*, 2:362.)

Miller, Thomas Benton. Born about 1842 in Ohio. Residence Mount Pleasant. Enlisted 16 September 1861, as Fourth Sergeant. Mustered in 15 October 1861. Re-enlisted and re-mustered 1 January 1864. Taken prisoner 21 March 1865. Mustered out 15 June 1865 at Davenport, Iowa. Died 19 July 1924 at Deer River, Itasca County, Minnesota. (*Roster and Record*, 2:362; Thomas B. Miller, *Organization Index to Pension Files of Veterans who served between 1861 and 1900;* cemetery records.)

Miller, William A. Born 17 February 1824 in Kentucky. Residence Panora, Guthrie County. Enlisted and mustered in 27 September 1864. Mustered out 2 June 1865, Washington, D. C. Died 1 August 1914 at Lathrop, Clinton County, Missouri. (*Roster and Record*, 2:362; William A. Miller, *Organization Index to Pension Files of Veterans who served between 1861 and 1900;* Clinton County, Missouri death certificate 25643, William A. Miller [1914], Missouri State Board of Health.)

Neally, Charles S. Born about 1845 in Iowa. Residence Muscatine County. Enlisted 5 October 1861, as Fifer. Mustered in 15 October 1861. Discharged for disability 5 June 1862 at Keokuk, Iowa. Died 18 March 1912. (*Roster and Record*, 2:366;

Charles S. Neally, *Organization Index to Pension Files of Veterans who served between 1861 and 1900.*)

Neel, James M. Born about 1838 in Indiana. Residence Mount Pleasant. Enlisted 16 September 1861. Mustered in 15 October 1861. Died 13 May 1862 of chronic diarrhea at Mount Pleasant, Iowa. (*Roster and Record*, 2:366; Baker, *Report of the Adjutant General*, 425; *Report of Brig.-Gen. Nathaniel B. Baker*, 639; cemetery records.)

Newman, Alney G. Born 10 October 1839 in Iowa. Residence Keosauqua, Van Buren County. Enlisted 26 August 1861. Mustered in 15 October 1861. Discharged for disability 7 February 1862 at Fulton, Missouri. Residence Birmingham. Enlisted 15 August 1862 in Company D, Thirtieth Infantry. Mustered in 31 August 1862. Mustered out 5 June 1865 at Washington, D. C. Died 4 May 1917 at Arkansas City, Cowley County, Kansas. (*Roster and Recod*, 2:366; Alney G. Newman, *Organization Index to Pension Files of Veterans who served between 1861 and 1900;* cemetery records.)

Nicodemus, William H. Born 23 August 1835 in Maryland. Residence Mount Pleasant. Enlisted 14 September 1861, as Fourth Corporal. Mustered in 15 October 1861. Promoted Third Corporal 6 November 1861. Re-enlisted and re-mustered 1 January 1864. Promoted Fourth Sergeant 9 November 1864; Third Sergeant 9 January 1865; Second Lieutenant 29 July 1865. Mustered out 15 July 1865 at Louisville, Kentucky. Died 4 May 1919 at Des Moines, Polk County, Iowa. (*Roster and Record*, 2:366; William H. Nicodemus, *Organization Index to Pension Files of Veterans who served between 1861 and 1900*; History of Appanoose County, Iowa [Chicago: Western Historical Co., 1878], 581.)

Nixon, John Francis. Born 8 June 1842 in Ohio. Residence Mount Pleasant. Enlisted 16 September 1861. Mustered in 15 October 1861. Re-enlisted and re-mustered 1 January 1864. Mustered out 15 July 1865 at Louisville, Kentucky. Died 2 November 1911 at St. Louis, Missouri. (*Roster and Record*, 2:366; John F. Nixon, *Organization Index to Pension Files of Veterans* *who served between 1861 and 1900;* St. Louis, Missouri death certificate no. 39256, John Francis Nixon [1911], Missouri State Board of Health.)

Ort, Christopher. Born about 1824 in Germany. Residence Panora, Guthrie County. Enlisted and mustered in 27 September 1864. Mustered out 20 May 1865 at Davenport, Iowa. Died 15 August 1870 at Panora, Guthrie County, Iowa. (*Roster and Record*, 2:368; cemetery records.)

Pallet, Theodore. Born about 1840 in Virginia. Residence Port Louisa, Louisa County. Enlisted 9 October 1861. Mustered in 15 October 1861. Killed in battle 6 April 1862 at Shiloh, Tennessee. Buried in Shiloh National Cemetery, Site 2059. (*Roster and Record*, 2:371; Baker, *Report of the Adjutant General*, 426; cemetery records.)

Paxton, Mathias. Born about 1837 in Ohio. Residence Rome, Henry County. Enlisted 9 September 1861. Mustered in 15 October 1861. Missing in action 26 July 1864 near Atlanta, Georgia. Mustered out 15 April 1865 at Annapolis, Maryland. Died 22 July 1924 at Rome, Henry County, Iowa. (*Roster and Record*, 2:371; Mathias Paxton, *Organization Index to Pension Files of Veterans who served between 1861 and 1900.*)

Pencil, George W. Born 20 May 1838 in Ohio. Residence Mount Pleasant. Enlisted 9 September 1861. Mustered in 15 October 1861. Discharged for disability 25 November 1862 at Grand Junction, Tennessee. Died 16 November 1920 at Ottumwa, Wapello County, Iowa. (*Roster and Record*; 2:371; Baker, *Report of the Adjutant General*, 426; George Pencil, *Organization Index to Pension Files of Veterans who served between 1861 and 1900*; cemetery records.)

Poor, Henry F. Born about 1838 in Indiana. Residence Mount Pleasant. Enlisted 15 September 1861. Mustered in 15 October 1861. Missing in action and taken prisoner 22 July 1864 near Atlanta, Georgia. Died 25 May 1865 at Annapolis, Maryland. Buried in Annapolis National Cemetery, Section C, Site 1116.

(*Roster and Record*, 2:371; Henry F. Pore, *Organization Index to Pension Files of Veterans who served between 1861 and 1900;* cemetery records; 1860 U.S. census, Henry Co., Iowa, Jackson twp., p. 390, Chancy Poore.)

Pound, Joseph D. Born about 1839 in New York. Residence Cedar County. Enlisted 3 October 1861. Mustered in and transferred to Company B 15 October 1861. Died of typhoid fever 23 January 1862 at California, Missouri. (*Roster and Record*, 2:369, 371.)

Richardson, James. Born about 1833 in Ohio. Residence Keosauqua, Van Buren County. Enlisted 4 September 1861. Mustered in 15 October 1861. Wounded in left hand severely 22 July 1864, near Atlanta, Georgia. Mustered out 18 October 1864 at Davenport, Iowa. (*Roster and Record*, 2:377; 1900 U.S. census, Warren Co., Iowa, Richland twp., p. 124-B, James Richardson.)

Richie, Chester C. Born about 1824 in Illinois. Residence Mount Pleasant. Enlisted 9 September 1861. Mustered in 15 October 1861. Discharged 16 April 1862 at St. Louis, Missouri. Buried in Pepin County, Wisconsin. (*Roster and Record*, 2:377; cemetery records.)

Riggs, Warren H. Born 5 October 1837 in Ohio. Residence Mount Pleasant. Enlisted 11 September 1861. Mustered in 15 October 1861. Promoted Hospital Steward 1 July 1863. Discharged 17 October 1864 at Chattanooga, Tennessee. Died 24 January 1910 in Washington County, Kansas. (*Roster and Record*, 2:377; Warren H. Riggs, *Organization Index to Pension Files of Veterans who served between 1861 and 1900;* cemetery records.)

Ross, William. Born about 1831 in Indiana. Residence Mount Pleasant. Enlisted 12 September 1861, as Fifth Sergeant. Mustered in 15 October 1861. Discharged for disability 28 April 1862 at Pittsburg Landing, Tennessee. Enlisted 4 January 1864 in Company D, Fourth Iowa Cavalry. Mustered out 8 August 1865 at Atlanta, Georgia. (*Roster and Record*, 2:377, 4:793.)

Rowley, Lacy J. Born about 1835 in Ohio. Residence Fort Dodge, Webster County. Enlisted and mustered in 29 September 1864. Died 21 November 1864 at Chattanooga, Tennessee. Buried in Chattanooga National Cemetery, Section G, Site 8296. (*Roster and Record*, 2:377 [Lacey J. Rowly]; Lacy J. Rowlee, *Organization Index to Pension Files of Veterans who served between 1861 and 1900;* cemetery records.)

Saums, Conrad. Born 2 October 1840 in Pennsylvania. Residence Mount Pleasant. Enlisted 12 September 1861. Mustered in 15 October 1861. Transferred to Mississippi Marine Brigade 6 April 1863. Died 23 March 1892 in Henry County, Iowa. (*Roster and Record*, 2:384; Conrad Sauns, *Organization Index to Pension Files of Veterans who served between 1861 and 1900;* cemetery records.)

Schreiner, Charles Julius. Born about 1839 in Ohio. Residence Mount Pleasant. Enlisted 10 October 1861. Mustered in 15 October 1861. Mustered out 17 October 1864 at Gaylesville, Alabama. Died 3 June 1907 at Mt. Pleasant, Henry County, Iowa. (*Roster and Record*, 2:384; Baker, *Report of the Adjutant General*, 426; Charles J. Schreiner, *Organization Index to Pension Files of Veterans who served between 1861 and 1900*; *History of Henry County, Iowa* [Chicago: Western Historical Co., 1879], 573; cemetery records.)

Semen, Providence M. Born about 1837 in Virginia. Residence Rome, Henry County. Enlisted 20 September 1861. Mustered in 15 October 1861. Died of chronic diarrhea 28 July 1863 at Corinth, Mississippi. (*Roster and Record*, 2:384; 1860 U.S. census, Henry Co., Iowa, Tippecanoe twp., Rome p. o., p. 358, G W Seaman.)

Serviss, George A. Born about 1843 in New York. Residence Mount Pleasant. Enlisted 5 October 1861. Mustered in 15 October 1861. Discharged for disability 23 November 1862, Grand Junction, Tennessee. Died 12 August 1898 in Dodge County, Nebraska. (*Roster and Record*, 2:384; George A, Serviss,

Organization Index to Pension Files of Veterans who served between 1861 and 1900; cemetery records.)

Shanks, Robert. Born 1 November 1833 in Indiana. Residence Panora, Guthrie County. Enlisted and mustered in 26 September 1864. Mustered out 2 June 1865, Washington, D. C. Died 10 March 1920 at Lathrop, Clinton County, Missouri. (*Roster and Record*, 2:384; Robert Shanks, *Organization Index to Pension Files of Veterans who served between 1861 and 1900;* Clinton County, Missouri death certificate no. 11991, Robert Shanks (1920), Missouri State Board of Health.)

Sharp, Robert J. Born 10 March 1842 in Iowa. Residence Mount Pleasant. Enlisted 11 September 1861. Mustered in 15 October 1861. Re-enlisted and re-mustered as Fourth Corporal 1 January 1864. Promoted to Second Corporal 9 November 1864 and to First Corporal 1 January 1865. Mustered out 15 June 1865 at Davenport, Iowa. Died 25 September 1887 in Clackamas County, Oregon. (*Roster and Record*, 2:384; Robert J. Sharp, *Organization Index to Pension Files of Veterans who served between 1861 and 1900;* cemetery records.)

Shaw, Rawley. Born 7 August 1835 in Preston County, Virginia. Residence Vernon, Van Buren County. Enlisted 17 September 1861, as Sixth Corporal. Mustered in 15 October 1861. Discharged for disability 18 June 1862 at Corinth, Mississippi. Died 20 August 1867 at the Federal hospital at Keokuk, Iowa. (*Roster and Record*, 2:384; Dale Walter, *Wilhelm and Simon Walter Family and Allied Families: the Story of a Family's Movement from Pennsylvania, Maryland, and West Virginia* [1999].)

Shaw, William. Born 16 September 1838 in Preston County, Virginia. Residence Keosauqua, Van Buren County. Enlisted 7 November 1861. Mustered in 12 November 1861. Mustered out 11 November 1864. Died 27 June 1910 in McPherson County, Kansas. (*Roster and Record*, 2:384; William Shaw, *Organization Index to Pension Files of Veterans who served between 1861 and*

1900; Walter, *Wilhelm and Simon Walter Family and Allied Families*.)

Sheets, William H. Born about 1842 in Ohio. Residence Mount Pleasant. Enlisted and mustered in 18 October 1861. Died 11 February 1862 at Fulton, Missouri. (*Roster and Record*, 2:384.)

Shipley, Samuel H. Born 1842 in Indiana. Residence Keosauqua, Van Buren County. Initially rejected by mustering officer 15 October 1861. Re-enlisted and re-mustered 1 January 1864. Mustered out 15 July 1865 at Louisville, Kentucky. Died 1908 in Van Buren County, Iowa (*Roster and Record*, 2:384; cemetery records.)

Siberts, Edward. Born 14 August 1834 in Pennsylvania. Residence Winfield, Henry County. Enlisted 17 September 1861. Mustered in 15 October 1861. He captured the flag of the Forty-fifth Alabama at Atlanta on 22 July 1864. Mustered out 17 October 1864 at Gaylesville, Alabama. Died 3 August 1895 at Winfield, Henry County, Iowa. (*Roster and Record*, 2:281, 384; Edward Siberts, *General Index to Pension Files of Veterans, 1861-1934*; cemetery records.)

Simpson, John H. Born about 1837 in Ohio. Residence Mount Pleasant. Enlisted 7 October 1861. Mustered in 15 October 1861. Discharged 8 January 1864, to enlist in Tenth Ohio Battery. Appointed Corporal 5 January 1865; reduced 24 April 1865. Mustered out with the battery 17 July 1865 at Camp Dennison, Ohio. (*Roster and Record*, 2:384; *Official Roster of the Soldiers of the State of Ohio in the War of the Rebellion, 1861-1866*, 10:521, 530.)

Smith, Charles Alvord. Born 29 February 1828 in Lake County, Ohio. Residence Mount Pleasant. Enlisted and mustered in 27 August 1862. Missing in action 22 July 1864 near Atlanta, Georgia. Mustered out 2 June 1865 at Washington, D. C. Died 17 November 1905 in Wayne township, Henry County, Iowa. (*Roster and Record*, 2:385; C. A. Smith, *Recollections of Prison Life at*

Andersonville, Georgia and Florence, South Carolina, Steven Fenton, ed. [Raleigh, N. C.: Martini Print Media, 1997], 104-107.)

Smith, Eli. Born about 1846 in Iowa. Residence Center Township, Henry County. Enlisted March, 1864. Mustered in 22 April 1864. Mustered out 15 July 1865 at Louisville, Kentucky. (*Roster and Record*, 2:385.)

Smith, James W. Born 7 July 1833 in Pennsylvania. Residence Davenport, Scott County. Enlisted 25 September 1861. Mustered in 15 October 1861. Re-enlisted and re-mustered 1 January 1864. Mustered out 15 July 1865 at Louisville, Kentucky. Died 6 February 1908 in Clay County, Nebraska. (*Roster and Record*, 2:385; James W. Smith, *Organization Index to Pension Files of Veterans who served between 1861 and 1900;* cemetery records.)

Smith, Marsilon. Born about 1842 in New York. Residence Mount Pleasant. Enlisted 16 September 1861. Mustered in 15 October 1861. Died of smallpox 11 February 1862 at Fulton, Missouri. (*Roster and Record*, 2:385)

Snively, William. Born about 1845 in Iowa. Residence Muscatine County. Enlisted 25 March 1864. Mustered in 28 March 1864. Mustered out 15 July 1865 at Louisville, Kentucky. Died 14 April 1920 at New Boston, Mercer County, Illinois. (*Roster and Record*, 2:385; William Snively, *Organization Index to Pension Files of Veterans who served between 1861 and 1900; Roster and Record*, 2:385.)

Southwick, Albert H. Born about 1840 in New York. Residence New Sharon, Mahaska County. Enlisted 12 September 1861. Mustered in and transferred to Company B 15 October 1861. Mustered out 17 October 1864 at Davenport, Iowa. Died 4 December 1918 at the National Soldiers Home, Los Angeles, California. Buried in Los Angeles National Cemetery, Section 37, Row F, Site 1. (*Roster and Record*, 2:385; Albert H. Southwick, *Organization Index to Pension Files of Veterans who served between 1861 and 1900*; cemetery records)

Springer, Abraham J. Born about 1841 in Russia. Residence Burlington, Des Moines County. Mustered in 15 October 1861. Re-enlisted and re-mustered 1 January 1864. Mustered out 15 July 1865, Louisville, Kentucky. Died 16 October 1885, buried in Sacramento, California. (Abraham Springer, *Organization Index to Pension Files of Veterans who served between 1861 and 1900;* cemetery records.)

Street, William N. Born about 1839 in Canada. Residence Millersburg, Iowa County. Enlisted 23 September 1861. Mustered in and transferred to Company B 15 October 1861. Wounded slightly in arm 6 April 1862 at Shiloh, Tennessee. Re-enlisted and re-mustered 1 January 1864. Wounded and taken prisoner 22 July 1864 near Atlanta, Georgia. (*Roster and Record*, 2:380, 385)

Stubbs, Martin D. Born 8 April 1837 in Indiana. Residence Mount Pleasant. Enlisted 20 September 1861. Mustered in 15 October 1861. Mustered out 17 October 1864 at Gaylesville, Alabama. Died 31 August 1867 in Henry County, Iowa. (*Roster and Record*, 2:385; Martin D. Stubbs, *Organization Index to Pension Files of Veterans who served between 1861 and 1900;* cemetery records.)

Stults, Ephraim Hall. Born 29 August 1844 in Indiana. Residence Mount Pleasant. Enlisted and mustered in 15 October 1861. Re-enlisted and re-mustered 1 January 1864. Mustered out 15 July 1865 at Louisville, Kentucky. Died 3 December 1930 at El Reno, Canadian County, Oklahoma. (*Roster and Record* 2:385; 1860 U.S. census, Henry Co., Iowa, Marion twp., Mt. Pleasant p. o, p. 333, W W Stultz; Ephraim Stults, *Organization Index to Pension Files of Veterans who served between 1861 and 1900*; cemetery records.)

Stults, George F. Born about 1848 in Indiana. Residence Center Township. Enlisted and mustered in 16 March 1864. Wounded in both legs severely 22 July 1864 near Atlanta, Georgia. Mustered out 15 July 1865 at Louisville, Kentucky. Died 21 February 1912 in Iowa. (*Roster and Record*, 2:385; 1860 U.S. census, Henry Co., Iowa, Marion twp., Mt. Pleasant p. o., p. 333, W W Stultz; George

F. Stults, *Organization Index to Pension Files of Veterans who served between 1861 and 1900.*)

Turney, Darius. Born about 1845 in Iowa. Residence Mount Pleasant. Enlisted 2 September 1861. Mustered in 15 October 1861. Re-enlisted and re-mustered 1 January 1864. Promoted Sixth Corporal 13 May 1864; Fourth Corporal 9 November 1864; Third Corporal 1 January 1865. Mustered out 15 July 1865 at Louisville, Kentucky. Died 12 July 1930 at Ceresco, Saunders County, Nebraska. (Baker, *Report of the Adjutant General*, 426; *Roster and Record*, 2:397; 1860 U.S. census, Henry Co., Iowa, Jefferson twp., Marshall p.o., p. 7, Danl Turney; Darius Turney, *Organization Index to Pension Files of Veterans who served between 1861 and 1900.*)

Vandervort, William A. Born about 1842 in Iowa. Residence Port Louisa, Louisa County. Enlisted 9 October 1861. Mustered in 15 October 1861. Died of consumption 9 February 1863 at Jackson, Tennessee. (*Roster and Record*, 2:398.)

Wade, William L. Enlisted 13 September 1861. Mustered in 15 Oct 1861. Promoted Seventh Corporal 17 April 1863. Reduced in ranks 1 January 1864. Mustered out 17 October 1864 at Gaylesville, Alabama. (*Roster and Record*, 2:400.)

Walter(s), Jacob. Born about 1839 in Pennsylvania. Residence Mount Pleasant. Enlisted 9 September 1861. Mustered in 15 October 1861. Discharged 18 October 1864 at Davenport, Iowa. Enlisted 31 January 1865 in Company D, 78 Pennsylvania Infantry. Residence at that time, Mechanicsburg, Pennsylvania. Mustered in 8 February 1865. Promoted to Sergeant 7 July 1865. Mustered out 11 September 1865. (*Roster and Record*, 2:400-401; Jacob Walters, *General Index to Pension Files of Veterans, 1861-1934*; *Civil War Veterans' Card File, 1861-1866 Indexes*, Pennsylvania State Archives.)

Walter, Rufus C. Born about 1842 in Pennsylvania. Residence Mount Pleasant. Enlisted 6 September 1861. Mustered in 15 October 1861. Died of dysentery 15 August 1863 at Vicksburg,

Mississippi. Buried in Vicksburg National Cemetery, Section G, Grave 173. (*Roster and Record*, 2:401).

Weir, Caleb B. Born 13 September 1837 in Washington County, Pennsylvania. Residence Mount Pleasant. Enlisted 2 September 1861, as First Sergeant. Mustered in 15 October 1861. Promoted Second Lieutenant 13 June 1862; First Lieutenant 1 January 1863. Resigned 27 June 1864. Died 24 August 1864 in Lee County, Iowa. (Baker, *Report of the Adjutant General*, 424; *Official Army Register of the Volunteer Force of the United States Army*, 7 pts. [Washington, D.C.: Adjutant General's Office, 1867] 7:263; *Roster and Record*, 2:401; cemetery records.)

White, Hiram A. Born about 1836 in Philadelphia, Pennsylvania. Residence Muscatine. Enlisted 18 April 1861 in Company A, First Iowa Infantry. Mustered in 14 May 1861. Mustered out 21 August 1861. Enlisted 5 October 1861, as Drummer. Mustered in 15 October 1861. Mustered out 17 October 1864 at Gaylesville, Alabama. Died 10 February 1928 at Marshalltown, Marshall County, Iowa. (Baker, *Report of the Adjutant General*, 424; *Roster and Record*, 1:82, 2:401; Hiram A. White, *Organization Index to Pension Files of Veterans who served between 1861 and 1900*; death notice, *Muscatine Journal and News-Tribune*, Muscatine, Iowa, 14 February 1928, p. 4.)

Wiley, George W. born 7 August 1839 in Morgan County, Ohio. Residence Keosauqua, Van Buren County. Enlisted 15 September 1861. Mustered in 15 October 1861. Re-enlisted and re-mustered 1 January 1864. Promoted Fifth Corporal 9 November 1864; Fourth Corporal 1 January 1865. Mustered out 15 July 1865 at Louisville, Kentucky. Died 22 December 1909 at Seneca, Nemaha County, Kansas. (*Roster and Record*, 2:401 [George Wyley]; George Wiley, *Organization Index to Pension Files of Veterans who served between 1861 and 1900;* cemetery records.)

Winder, Thomas C. Born 8 January 1842 in Harrison County, Ohio. Residence Port Louisa, Louisa County. Enlisted and mustered in 17 October 1861. Mustered out 17 October 1864 at Gaylesville, Alabama. Died 8 April 1925 at Anita, Cass County,

Iowa. (*Roster and Record*, 2:401; *History of Cass County, Iowa* [Springfield, Ill.: Continental Historical Co., 1884], 642-643; Thomas C. Winder, *Organization Index to Pension Files of Veterans who served between 1861 and 1900*; cemetery records.)

Woodworth, Omri. Born 20 August 1829 in Ashtabula County, Ohio. Residence Mount Pleasant. Enlisted 16 September 1861. Mustered in 15 October 1861. Mustered out 17 October 1864 at Gaylesville, Alabama. Died 1 October 1909 in Page County, Iowa. (*Roster and Record*, 2:401; *Biographical History of Page County, Iowa* [Chicago: Lewis & Dunbar, 1890], 685-686; Omri Woodworth, *Organization Index to Pension Files of Veterans who served between 1861 and 1900;* cemetery records.)

Woodworth, John B. Born 1838 in Illinois. Residence Mount Pleasant. Enlisted 16 September 1861. Mustered in 15 October 1861. Promoted Eighth Corporal 1 July 1862. Mustered out 17 October 1864 at Gaylesville, Alabama. Died 1907 in El Paso County, Colorado. (*Roster and Record*, 2:401; John B. Woodworth, *Organization Index to Pension Files of Veterans who served between 1861 and 1900;* cemetery records.)

Wooley, David. Born 28 April 1828 in Indiana. Residence Mount Pleasant. Enlisted 16 September 1861. Mustered in 15 October 1861. Re-enlisted and re-mustered 1 January 1864. Mustered out 15 July 1865, Louisville, Kentucky. Died 30 October 1899 at the National Soldiers Home, Los Angeles, California. Buried in Los Angeles National Cemetery, Section 5, Row C, Site 1. (*Roster and Record*, 2:401; David Woolley, *Organization Index to Pension Files of Veterans who served between 1861 and 1900;* cemetery records.)

Yeager, Joseph. Born 18 August 1839 in Ohio. Residence Mount Pleasant. Enlisted 16 September 1861. Mustered in 15 October 1861. Wounded in left shoulder severely 22 July 1864 near Atlanta, Georgia. Mustered out 17 October 1864 at Gaylesville, Alabama. Died 26 May 1895 in Union County, Iowa. (*Roster and Record*, 2:404; Joseph Yeager, *Organization Index to Pension*

Files of Veterans who served between 1861 and 1900; cemetery records.)

Bibliography

Manuscript Collections

Diaries of Mifflin Jennings, Co. C, Eleventh Iowa Infantry, MS, originals in the possession of Ronald D. Smith, Larned, Kansas.

William S. Fultz, "A History of Company D, Eleventh Iowa Infantry Volunteers," MS, Special Collections, State Historical Society of Iowa, Iowa City, Iowa.

Published Works

Ambrose, Stephen E., *Halleck: Lincoln's Chief of Staff* (Baton Rouge: Louisiana State University Press, 1962).

Ballard, Michael, *Vicksburg: the Campaign that Opened the Mississippi* (Chapel Hill: University of North Carolina Press, 2004).

Biographical History of Page County, Iowa (Chicago: Lewis & Dunbar, 1890).

Biographical Record and Portrait Album of Tippecanoe County, Indiana (Chicago: Lewis, 1888).

Biographical Review of Henry County, Iowa (Chicago: Hobart Publishing, 1906).

Bonds, Russell S., *War Like the Thunderbolt: the Battle and Burning of Atlanta* (Yardley, Pennsylvania: Westholme, 2009).

Branch, Carolyn Paul, Fulton, *Missouri 1820-1920: a History in Stories and Photographs* (Longbranch Press, 2010).

Brigham, Johnson, *Iowa: Its History and Its Foremost Citizens* (Chicago: Clarke, 1918).

Burge, William, *Through the Civil War and Western Adventures* (Lisbon, Ia.: W. Burge, n. d.).

Byers, S. H. M., *Iowa in War Times* (Des Moines: W. D. Condit, 1888).

Cardwell, Dr. Mae H., "The Oregon State Medical Society -- an Historical Sketch," *Medical Sentinel,* v. 13, no. 7 (July 1905).

Castel, Albert, *Decision in the West: the Atlanta Campaign of 1864* (Lawrence: University of Kansas Press, 1992).

Cemetery Records, Franklin Township, Hendricks County, Indiana (Danville, Ind.: County Seat Genealogical Society, 2004).

Clark, Olynthus B., ed., *Downing's Civil War Diary* (Des Moines: Historical Department of Iowa, 1916).
Clark, Dan Elbert, *Samuel Jordan Kirkwood* (Iowa City: State Historical Society of Iowa, 1917).

Compact Edition of the Oxford English Dictionary (Oxford University Press, 1971).

Conard, Howard L., *Encyclopedia of the History of Missouri: a Compendium of History and Biography for Ready Reference*, 6 vols.(New York: Southern History Co., 1901).

Cooper-Wiele, Jonathan K., *Skim Milk Yankees Fighting: the Battle of Athens, Missouri, August 5, 1861* (Iowa City: Camp Pope Bookshop, 2007).

Cozzens, Peter, *The Darkest Days of the War: The Battles of Iuka and Corinth* (Chapel Hill: University of North Carolina Press, 1997).

Cunningham, O. Edward, *Shiloh and the Western Campaign of 1862* (New York: Savas Beatie, 2007).

Daniel, Larry J., *Shiloh: the Battle that Changed the Civil War* (New York: Touchstone, 1997).

Dictionary of American Naval Fighting Ships, 8 vols. (Washington, D.C.: Government Printing Office, 1959-1981).

Eicher, David J., *The Longest Night: a Military History of the Civil War* (New York: Simon & Schuster, 2001).

Eicher, John H., and David J. Eicher, *Civil War High Commands* (Stanford, Calif.: Stanford University Press, 2001).

Everett, Frank E., Jr., *A History of the First Presbyterian Church of Vicksburg in the Nineteenth Century* (Vicksburg: 1980).

Foster, Buck T., *Sherman's Mississippi Campaign* (Tuscaloosa: University of Alabama Press, 2006).

Garrison, Webb, *The Encyclopedia of Civil War Usage: an Illustrated Compendium of the Everyday Language of Soldiers and Civilians* (Nashville:Cumberland House, 2001).

"General Alexander Chambers," *Iowa Historical Record* 9:1 (January 1893), 385-393.

Gresham, Matilda, *Life of Walter Quintin Gresham, 1832-1895* (Chicago: Rand McNally, 1919).

Gue, Benjamin F., *History of Iowa: From the Earliest Times to the Beginning of the Twentieth Century*, 4 vols. (New York: Century History Co., 1903).

Guinn, James M., *Historical and Biographical Record of Los Angeles and Vicinity* (Chicago: Chapman, 1901).

Hare, Linda Alstrom, *Seven Hares in the Civil War* (Atlanta, Kan.: HHR, 2005).

Hearn, Chester G., *Ellet's Brigade: the Strangest Outfit of All* (Baton Rouge: Louisiana State University Press, 2000).

Heiss, Willard, ed., *Abstracts of the Records of the Society of Friends in Indiana*, 6 pts.(Indianapolis: Indiana Historical Society, 1962-1975).

History of Des Moines County, Iowa (Chicago: Western Historical Co., 1879).

History of Henry County, Iowa (Chicago: Western Historical Co., 1879).

Hubbart, Phillip A., ed., *An Iowa Soldier Writes Home: the Civil War Letters of Union Private Daniel J. Parvin* (Durham, N. C.: Carolina Academic Press, 2011).

Illustrated History of Los Angeles County, California, (Chicago: Lewis Publishing Co., 1889).

Ingersoll, Lurton Dunham, *Iowa and the Great Rebellion* (Philadelphia: Lippincott, 1866).

Iowa Adjutant General's Office, *Report of Brig.-Gen. Nathaniel B. Baker, Adjutant General and Act'g Q.M.G. and Act'g as P.M.G...*, 2 vols. (Des Moines, 1867).

Iowa Adjutant General's Office, *Roster and Record of Iowa Soldiers in the War of the Rebellion*, 6 vols., (Des Moines, 1909-1911).

Jennings, William Henry, *My Story* (Fremont, Neb.: Hammond Printing Co., c. 1915).

Lael, Richard L., et al., *Evolution of a Missouri Asylum: Fulton State Hospital, 1851-2006* (Columbia, Mo.: University of Missouri Press, 2007).

McDonough, James L., and James Pickett Jones, *War So Terrible: Sherman and Atlanta* (New York: Norton, 1987).

McElroy, John, *The Struggle for Missouri* (Washington, D.C.: National Tribune, 1909).

Memorial and Biographical Record of Iowa Illustrated (Chicago: Lewis Publishing Co., 1896).

Michaels, Edward Rynearson, (ed.), *The Civil War Letters of Sylvester Rynearson, 1861-1865* (E. R. Michaels, 1981).

Newell, Isaac D., *History of the Ram Fleet and the Mississippi Marine Brigade in the War for the Union* (St. Louis: Buschart, 1907).

Perrin, William Henry, *History of Effingham County, Illinois* (Chicago: O. L. Baskin & Co., 1883).

Portrait and Biographical Record of Dubuque, Jones and Clayton Counties, Iowa (Chicago: Chapman, 1894).

Portrait and Biographical Album of Henry County, Iowa (Chicago: Acme, 1888).

Portrait and Biographical Album of Des Moines County, Iowa (Chicago: Acme Publishing, 1888).

"Recollections of Crocker's Iowa Brigade," *Iowa Historical Record*, v. 1, no. 3 (July 1885), 129-132.

Reed, Richard D., *Historic MSD: the story of the Missouri School for the Deaf* (Fulton, Mo.: Richard D. Reed, 2000).

Scott, William Forse, *The Story of a Cavalry Regiment: The Career of the Fourth Iowa Veteran Volunteers* (New York: Putnam, 1893).

Shea, John Gilmary, *A Child's History of the United States* (New York: McDavitt, 1872).

Shea, William L., and Earl J. Hess, *Pea Ridge: Civil War Campaign in the West* (Chapel Hill: University of North Carolina Press, 1992).

Shepherd, Rebecca A., et al., *A Biographical Directory of the Indiana General Assembly* (Indianapolis: Select Committee on the Centennial History of the Indiana General Assembly: Indiana Historical Bureau, 1980).

Smith, C. A., *Recollections of Prison Life at Andersonville, Georgia and Florence, South Carolina*, Steven Fenton, ed. (Raleigh, N. C.: Martini Print Media, 1997).

Soley, James Russell, *Admiral Porter* (New York: Appleton, 1903).

Story of the Fifty-fifth Regiment Illinois Volunteer Infantry in the Civil War 1861-1865 (Clinton, Mass.: Coulter, 1887).

Stuart, Addison A., *Iowa Colonels and Regiments* (Des Moines: Mills, 1865).

Temple, Seth, "Camp McClellan during the Civil War," *Annals of Iowa*, 21:1(July 1937).

Throne, Mildred, ed., "A History of Company D, Eleventh Iowa Infantry, 1861-1865," *Iowa Journal of History*, v. 55, no. 1 (January 1957), 35-90

Thompson, S. D., *Recollections with the Third Iowa Regiment* (Cincinnati, 1864).

Twain, Mark, *Life on the Mississippi* (New York: Harper & Row, 1965).

United States War Department, *The War of the Rebellion: Official Records of the Union and Confederate Armies*, 128 vols. (Washington D.C.: Government Printing Office, 1881-1901).

Wakelyn, Jon L., *Biographical Dictionary of the Confederacy* (Westport, Conn.: Greenwood, 1977).

Walter, Dale, *Wilhelm and Simon Walter Family and Allied Families: the Story of a Family's Movement from Pennsylvania, Maryland and West Virginia* (1999).

War of the Rebellion: a Compilation of the Official Records of the Union and Confederate Armies (Washington, D.C.: Government printing Office, 1880-1901).

Warner, Ezra J., *Generals in Gray* (Baton Rouge: Louisiana State University Press, 1959).

Warner, Ezra J., *Generals in Blue: Lives of the Union Commanders* (Louisiana State University Press, 1964).
Wheeler, William Ogden, *The Ogden family in America* (1997).

Whittelsey, Charles Barney, *Genealogy of the Whittlesey-Whittelsey Family* (New York: Whittlesey House, 1941).

Winters, John D., *The Civil War in Louisiana* (Baton Rouge: Louisiana State University Press, 1963).

Woodworth, Steven E., *Nothing But Victory: the Army of the Tennessee, 1861-1865* (New York: Vintage Books, 2005).

Index

Abercrombie, John C., *64*, 72, 106
Acworth Station, Ga., 128
Adairsville, Ga., 129
Allatoona Pass, Ga., 128
Alpine, Ga., 130
Anderson, Capt. John W., 133

Baker, Nathaniel B., 74, 75n
Barr, David H., 26, 136
Barr, George W. F., 4, 129, 136
Bayou Macon, La., 91
Beeler, John, 87, 88n, 136-137
Belknap, Gen. William W., 129
Big Black River, Miss., 73, 77, 81, 83
Black, William, 37, 38, 137
Bledsoe, Benjamin H., 22, 137
Boeuf River, La., 90, 91
Bolivar, Tenn., 50
Boonesboro, Mo., 16
Boonville, Mo., 16
Bourne (Bohn), Capt. William F., 118, 134
Brazelton House Hotel, Mt. Pleasant, Ia., 4
Buck, Sgt. John A., 134

Cairo, Ill., 32

Camp Benton, Mo., 9, 32
Camp McClellan, Davenport, Ia., 5
Campbell, Arch S., 10, *11*, 12, 13, 103, 128, 138
Cape Girardeau, Mo., 32
Cartersville, Ga., 128
Chambers, Col. Alexander, 6, 99
Chattahoochee River, Ga., 117
Chattanooga, Tenn., 131
Chattooga River, Ga., 130
Chewalla, Tenn., 49
Chickamauga, Ga., 131
Clinton, Miss., 82
Concord, Mo., 19
Corinth, Miss., 47, 51
Courtney, Joseph L., 87, 88n, 127, 139

Dailey, Francis M., 102, 140
Davis, Mr., 28
Dawson, Mr. (James), 40
Decatur, Ga., 117
Easton, Capt. Orlando W., 102
Edward's Station, Miss., 82
Elrod, Capt. John, 59, 60n
Etowa River, Ga., 128

Farley, Francis H. (Frank), 118

173

Flory, Francis M. (Frank), 78, 87, 141
Force, Franklin, 11, 106, 141-142
Fort Henry, Tenn., 32
Foster, Samuel, 21, 66, 87, 103, 116, 142
Fulton, Mo., 19, 20, 23, 29

Gaskill, Elis, 10, 142
Gaylesville, Ala., 130
Goodrich's Landing, La., 89
Grand Gulf, Miss., 70
Grant, Maj. Gen. Ulysses S., 71, 98
Greenville, Miss., 60
Gresham, Brig. Gen. Walter Q., 115

Haines Bluff, Miss., 71, 74
Hales, (Hugh B.) Americus, 56
Hale(s), (John) Clark, 35
Hall, Col. William, 8, 36, 115
Hard Times Landing, La., 70
Hare, Col. Abraham M., *15*, 20, 22
Harlan, Mrs. Senator (Ann Eliza Peck), 40
Harlan(d), David, 13
Hatchie River, Tenn., 49
Heald, William, 57, 143
Helena, Ark., 55
Hobert, Mortimer, 38, 143
Hoe, Frank (William F. Hough), 37

Holloway, Harrison, 119, 143-144
Hudson, Andrew J., 85, 86, 117, 144
Hummell, William, 57, 79, 96, 144-145

Iuka, Miss., 51

Jackson, Miss., 81
Jefferson City, Mo., 13, 17, 31
Jessup, Jonathan, 55, 56, *69*, 73, 98, 99
Jessup, Levi (Grandfather), 22, *25*, 26, 83, 88, 95, 99, 105, 107
Jessup, Samuel Merrill, *24*, 83
Jessup, Solon R., *86*, 104
Jonesboro, Ga., 123
Judah, Gen. Henry M., 43

Kauffman, John W., 26, 66, 145
Kendell, Jesse, 88, 145
Kennesaw Mountain, Ga., 127, 128
Kingsbury, Madison M., 97, 146
Kingston, Ga., 128
Kirkwood, Gov. Samuel J., 74

LaFayette, Ga., 130
Lafayette, Tenn., 53
Lake Providence, La., 59, 63
Lake St. Joseph, La., 70

Lehew, Lt. William F., 25, 147
Lockwood, Edwin J., 105, 147
Lovejoy Station, Ga., 123
Lowry, Ambrose, 10, 26, 148

Marietta, Ga., 116, 117, 127
Matthews, D. Wade, 54, 56, 57, 59, 74, 87, 100, 101, 102, 105, 106, 126, 128
Matthews, Dr. William, *101*
McArthur, Brig. Gen. John, 66, 72
McDowell, Charles, 40, 41n
McFarland, Capt. Samuel, 3, *4*, 18, 22, 148-149
McGavic, James, 84, 149
McKean, Brig. Gen. Thomas J., 14
McNeeley, George, 57, 107, 117, 149
McPherson, Maj. Gen. James B., 62, 71, 73, 97
Mechanicsburg, Miss., 73
Memphis, Tenn., 37
Messinger's Ferry or Ford, Miss., 77, 78
Middleton, Tenn., 49
Miller, Madison J. (Jay), 84, 151
Millersburg, Mo., 20
Milliken's Bend, La., 58, 67
Monroe, La., 90

Napolean, Ark., 56

Nashville, Tenn., 132
Neel, James M., 21, 152
New Carthage, La., 70
Nicodemus, William H., 105, 152

Paducah, Ky., 32
Pallett, Theodore, 37, 38, 153
Pencil, George, 21, 153
Pittsburg Landing, Tenn., 34
Pomutz (Pamootz), Maj. George, 94, *95*
Porter, Adm. David D., 71
Powder Springs, Ga., 127
Providence, Mo., 16
Purdy, Tenn., 44

Rawlins, Gen. John A., 36
Redbone, Miss., 107
Resaca, Ga., 129
Richardson, James, 86, 154
Richie, Chester C., 66, 154
Richmond, La., 67
Ro(w)ley, James F., 13-14

St. Louis, Mo., 9, 31, 32
Savannah, Tenn., 32, 33
Schreiner, Charles J. (Jule), 76, 155
Shane, Col. John, 57
Sharp, Robert J., 87, 94, 95, 104, 156
Shedd, Col. Warren, 133
Shiloh Church, Tenn., 34
Siberts, Edward, 105, 157
Snake Creek Gap, Ga., 129

Snoddy, Emily Jessup Wade (Mother), *83*, 87, 88, 89, 91, 96, 104, 106, 116, 118, 125, 126
Stanton, Maj. Thaddeus H., 87
Stevenson, Tenn., 132
Stone, Gov. Willam, 119
Strong, Maj. William E., 62
Stubbs, Martin D., 85, 86, 159
Summersville, Ga., 130

Tennessee River, Ky., 32
Tensas River, La., 90
Thomas, Adjutant Gen. Lorenzo, 62, *65*
Turney, Darius, 10, 13, 160
Tuttle, Gen. James M., 49

Vicksburg, Miss., 58, 71, 85, 91, 93, 100

Wade, Annie L., 62, 65, 89
Wade, Amelia, 25, 74, 82, 84, 86, 88, 91, 93, 95, 100, 103, 107, 125, 126, 128
Wade, Robert D., 85, 93, *94*, 104, 105, 128
Walter(s), Jacob, 25, 160
Walter(s), Rufus C., 25, 88, 160-161
Warrenton, Miss., 72
Watson, Dr. William, 27
Weir, Caleb B., 4, 67, 68, 161
Wentz, Col. August, 7
White, Hiram, 89, 128, 161

Winder, Thomas, 78, 129, 161-162
Woodworth, John B., 85, 86, 170
Woodworth, Omri, 85, 86, 170
Wooley, David, 87, 88n, 162

Yazoo River, Miss., 56, 71
Yeager, Joseph, 88, 162
Young's Point, La., 71

www.ingramcontent.com/pod-product-compliance
Lightning Source LLC
Chambersburg PA
CBHW072129160426
43197CB00012B/2041